BIRTH TO THREE

BIRTH TO THREE
A Self-Help Program for New Parents

ANDI FISCHHOFF

Castalia Publishing Company
Parent Education Division
P.O. Box 1587
Eugene, Oregon 97440

Fischhoff, Andi, 1947-
    Birth to Three.

    Includes bibliographies.
    1. Birth to Three (Organization : Eugene, Or.)
2. Parenting—Study and teaching—Oregon. 3. Self-help
groups—Oregon. I. Title.
HQ755.7.F57   1986   649'.1   86-6123
ISBN 0-916154-15-7 (pbk.)

ISBN: 0-916154-15-7
Printed in the United States of America

Copies of this book may be ordered from the publisher.

Editorial and Production Credits:
    Editor-in-Chief: Scot G. Patterson
    Copy Editor: Cheryl Brunette
    Editor's Assistant: Jina LaMear
    Typesetting and Layout: John Macioce
    Photography: Scot Patterson and Joanna Kishpaugh

Acknowledgements

Although my name appears as author of this book it has hardly been an individual effort. Foremost, the book is dedicated to Minalee Saks and Sue Kelly who co-founded this program with me. It is also a tribute to the other wonderful women with whom I've worked at Birth to Three: Rosalie Harris, Jo Hale Lyndon, Sylvia Lee Hanley, Betty Kellow, Juvata Rusch, Kyle Hopkins, Lois Newton, Sharon Whitlow, Sharon Paulsen, Carol Halverson, Robbie Wright, and Ruthann Maguire. Much gratitude is due also to Birth to Three's loyal Board of Directors, and to the many parents in Birth to Three groups from whom I've learned so much.

Thank you, Scot, for being such a patient and exacting editor.

A giant hug for my family. Baruch, thank you for your constant support and encouragement, sound advice, and marvelous editing—you are so appreciated. And special thanks to our kids, Maya, Ilya, and Noam; without you I'd probably have picked a different career altogether.

—Andi

Contents

An Introduction to Birth to Three

Babies—they can change your life completely. Sometimes just talking to other new parents can be awfully reassuring. Birth to Three is an organization that brings new parents together so they can share their parenting experiences, learn together, and give support to each other. At Birth to Three's core are support groups of eight to 10 new parents (and their babies) who live in the same neighborhood. The meetings follow a semistructured format and are run by a group leader who is also a parent of young children. Birth to Three groups reduce the isolation that so frequently accompanies the arrival of a new baby and provide a setting in which parents can learn about raising infants. By promoting good parenting skills and a positive attitude toward childrearing, Birth to Three helps parents gain confidence in their parenting skills, resolve problems, and enjoy parenting more.

Raising a baby is a demanding job for which few of us are adequately prepared. New parents have an immediate need

1

for *information* on a variety of topics. Often, that information is obtained haphazardly, by talking with family members, friends, and pediatricians, or by reading books and magazine articles. But many parents do not have friends or family who can give them advice, and seeing a pediatrician very often can be an expensive education. Moreover, once the baby is born it is no simple matter to find the time or energy for uninterrupted reading. Mountains of books and magazines are published each year on parenting and child development. Finding material that you need and enjoy can be a challenge to even the most literate and motivated parent. Contradictory advice from different sources may leave you wondering what to believe, eroding your self-confidence and inhibiting your flexibility.

New parents also need *support* to be effective caretakers. Adult companionship, encouragement, and help with routine household chores are more important than ever. Yet many mothers find themselves relatively isolated and confined to their homes with their newborns. Dropping in on friends requires more planning now that there is a baby, and many people stop coming by because they know that you are busy being a parent. This is unfortunate because mothers need social support. Support from other parents acts as a "buffer" for the stress associated with raising children, and helps reinvigorate a parent who may, at times, feel overwhelmed by the day-to-day work of childrearing.

In the past, the extended family served the function of providing both information and support for family members. With the wisdom of several generations at their disposal, new parents approached childrearing with all the advice and assistance they could handle. But things are different in today's mobile and rapidly changing society, and the extended family has often broken apart. As a result, many new parents feel very isolated. Under these circumstances, even small problems can become crises.

Birth to Three support groups are designed to meet the needs of new parents by bringing them together in a semi-structured educational setting. Parents themselves are a tremendous resource—by working together they can help each other to develop and refine their parenting skills and at the same time provide mutual support. But new parents typically do not have much contact with one another, hence the usefulness of an organization such as Birth to Three. Birth to Three support groups generally meet once every week or every other week, and may continue to meet for several years as new babies are born and new mothers join the group to replace those who leave. Although the participants in the groups are usually mothers, more and more fathers are becoming involved. The groups are organized by neighborhoods so that it is easy for members to see each other between meetings. Enduring friendships form as children play together and parents get to know one another.

Meetings are informal, and there is an opportunity for everyone to exchange personal news as well as discuss a topic of interest to the group. Occasionally a speaker may be invited to address the meeting. A specific focus is usually chosen for each meeting such as developmental stages in infancy or nutrition. Chapter 7 of this book has been designed to help group leaders choose appropriate topics and materials for discussion. Eight "units" have been developed on areas of most concern to new parents. These units can be used as a discussion outline for eight group meetings or parent education classes. Each unit features a short article written by a professional that provides an overview of the topic. A list of additional topics for discussion is presented in Appendix 7.1. Suggested readings are also provided along with an annotated reading list of books and magazines for further study. While each meeting has a theme, the leader must be flexible enough to allow the group to depart from the day's topic so that pressing issues can also be discussed.

Birth to Three is a practical program that was started in 1978 in Eugene, Oregon. Since then, the program has been enthusiastically received by parents and professionals in the community. Each year, over 700 parents participate in support groups and classes (including special classes for parents under stress and classes for adolescent parents). Although support groups and classes are the core of the program, we also provide additional services for new parents. Approximately 500 parents attend regularly scheduled educational events and about 1,200 parents each year call our peer-counseling "warm line" for support. It is estimated that a total of 10,000 peer-counseling calls are made by group leaders to members of their groups each year. The Birth to Three newsletter is received by 1,100 families bimonthly. The newsletter features articles on child development, book reviews, interviews, stories written by Birth to Three members, and information about relevant local events. Each year more than 3,500 new parents receive a Birth to Three poster describing community resources when they leave the hospital or birthing center with their newborns.

The rapid growth of Birth to Three in the Eugene area, at a time when other social services are diminishing, suggests that the program meets a real need. Self-help groups such as Birth to Three have become tremendously popular over the last few years. These groups offer participants an opportunity for personal development and create a sense of community. There is no distinction between "professional" and "client" because the roles of helper and helped are interchangeable. Everyone is recognized as having experienced problems and having acquired areas of expertise. We believe that parents of young children are in a perfect position to learn from each other, boost one another's confidence, and enhance the first years of childrearing through mutual support. Birth to Three also appeals to a wide range of parents because it does not endorse any one philosophy or orientation to parenting. No one is excluded because of his or her beliefs or approach to child-rearing. When we telephone new parents to invite them to participate in a group in their neighborhood, over half of them join!

This book has been written to provide step-by-step guidelines for setting up support groups and providing additional services to new parents in your community. A Birth to Three program can be organized in several different ways: 1) by one parent or a group of parents interested in forming a support group; 2) by a group of parents who want to create a community-wide program of classes, support groups, and other services to new parents; and 3) by health or mental health professionals organizing programs for new parents or training volunteers to do so. You can start an ambitious program or one that is less complicated. If your goal is a modest support group for you and your friends, there are sections of this book that may look formidable. Don't let yourself be intimidated—we learned as we went along, too.

This book will show you how to build on our experience to create Birth to Three groups in your area. Additional materials are available from our organization to help you get going. We are also willing to refer parents to other Birth to Three programs on request. For more information on joining or forming a group, see page 42. Given our success in Eugene with parents of widely different backgrounds, we believe that Birth to Three offers a useful model for parents everywhere.

While the primary function of this book is to provide guidelines for setting up parent support groups, it may also be of interest to parents and educators who do not intend to join or form groups. It can be used both as a source of information about parenting and as a guide to the literature for further study. Prospective parents can read this book on their own, or instructors teaching "Family Life" classes offered through Home Economics departments at high schools, universities, and community colleges can use it as a text.

Another important purpose of this book is to help parents understand that what they are experiencing is "normal." As new parents, many of us find it reassuring to read about other parents' thoughts, feelings, and experiences, especially when they admit to coping with problems that we recognize as our own. The statements from parents and descriptive material in the first two chapters of this book should strike a chord in almost every parent. Sometimes just reading about the perspective of other parents can help you to feel better about your own situation. (Reading what other parents have to say is not quite the same as having them to talk to, but it can help a lot.) We believe in a positive approach to parenting, but being a parent is not easy. The good times will take care of themselves. What we need is reassurance that the bad times will pass and help in making that happen.

Finally, this book outlines a program which is essentially a grassroots effort to prevent child abuse. According to the National Center on Child Abuse and Neglect, "homegrown, community-based and conceived programs aimed at bettering the lives of *all* families offer the most promise for primary prevention of child abuse and neglect, as well as for prevention of such related problems as delinquency and drug and alcohol abuse" *(Perspectives on Child Maltreatment in the Mid '80s,* U.S. Department of Health and Human Services). Birth to Three is such a program. As a primary prevention model, Birth to Three is available to all parents in the community, promoting positive attitudes toward childrearing, enhancing parents' self-esteem, and educating parents at a critical time when their children are small and patterns of interaction are being established. One of the most important things Birth to Three does is to encourage parents to ask for help when they need it. This is crucial because isolation is one of the factors associated with parents abusing their children. Birth to Three groups are neighborhood based, enabling parents to contact one another between meetings and establish the sorts of supportive contacts that extend well beyond the group's official meeting times.

Birth to Three originally received funding from the National Center on Child Abuse and Neglect as a child abuse prevention demonstration project. We all know that the costs to society of child abuse are enormous, and that treatment after the damage has been done is far less effective than prevention. Children who have been dealt with cruelly during the years in which they should have been nurtured grow up to repeat the pattern of violence and victimization with their own children. Birth to Three works with families to *prevent* the home situation from deteriorating to the point that a child-protective service agency must intervene. Ongoing peer-support groups are a very efficient way to deliver mental health services to large numbers of parents who must deal every day with the work of bringing up children. If these people were to seek low-cost professional counseling, they might have to wait weeks or longer for help. Parents who belong to a Birth to Three group always have somewhere to turn when things get out of hand—they can call their group leader, other parents in their group, or the peer-counseling "warm line" for help.

One might wonder why parent support groups don't form spontaneously more often if they are so valuable. Our experience suggests that new parents do not meet each other very easily. Because driving has replaced walking as the primary means of getting around, contact with other new parents may be limited to casual encounters in stores and doctors' waiting rooms. These settings are not the best place to have a good conversation or strike up a friendship. Even in the most gregarious community, it is better to invest time in organizing a group than to depend upon chance exchanges with other parents. It often takes a special setting to discuss the things that concern new parents most. Birth to Three can be that special setting.

What Parents and Professionals Say
About Birth to Three

Birth to Three has been enthusiastically received by parents and professionals in the local community and across the country. We survey parents in our groups regularly to find out if the program is working for them. The results of those surveys are presented here, as are comments from parents about what Birth to Three has meant to them. Endorsements from professionals who have worked with us and expressed support for the program are also included. From the very beginning, Birth to Three has solicited support from people in all sectors of the community. We are pleased that our program has received such an overwhelmingly positive response from the people who participate in it. We hope that Birth to Three organizations in other communities will benefit from the same sort of local support that has made our program flourish.

Questionnaire Results

Perhaps the most important question in our questionnaire is, "Would you recommend Birth to Three to other parents?" One-hundred percent of the parents participating in the survey answered that they would! Parents are also asked, "Do you feel better about your parenting as a result of being in a Birth to Three group?" Ninety-two percent of the parents responding to this question answered "yes." Another question asks parents to describe in their own words what they hoped to achieve by joining a group: "What were your goals in coming to Birth to Three?" The most common response was "to meet other mothers" (93%). When parents were asked if their goals had been met, 95% of them answered "yes." These results are very satisfying to us. It is reassuring to know that parents feel that the program is so effective in meeting their needs.

8

Statements from Parents

"It is hard to explain the loneliness, mixed with frustration and exhaustion, that a new mother—or, in my case, the mother of an infant and a toddler—feels in the months that follow the arrival of the baby. But this loneliness, which was doubled for me because I was new to the area, was almost eliminated by Birth to Three. From the time I delivered my baby—I was given a Birth to Three poster at the hospital—Birth to Three was in contact with me. This contact with the Birth to Three staff and my group—which has made me feel that I'm not alone in sometimes feeling overwhelmed by everything—has helped me become a member of the community and, I hope, a better parent. Finally, just to know that Birth to Three is there as a resource and, if you need it, someone to talk to is very comforting to me and other new parents."

a Birth to Three parent

"I am the mother of a beautiful three-month-old daughter. Her arrival into our family was eagerly anticipated. We planned and prepared. We received support from our family and friends, our church, our physician, the hospital, and our Lamaze group. This support continued for two or three weeks after her birth. Then, suddenly, we were on our own. We hadn't planned on or prepared for the confusion, frustration, and apprehension that often accompany new parenthood. At times I felt isolated and depressed. My husband seemed to be under a lot of pressure. I could see he was beginning to worry about the baby and me. Gradually our relationship to each other, and to our child, became less than satisfactory. Our little 'bundle of joy' was causing some

9

serious problems. . . . I have a master's degree in special education, and specialized in working with emotionally disturbed children. My husband is a physician in family practice. . . . We thought we knew everything parents could possibly need to know about successful parenting. We did not realize how much parents need other parents."

a Birth to Three parent

"For those of us without family in the area, the members of the group become our family. My 10-month-old daughter became quite ill recently. In the course of nursing her back to health I contracted pneumonia. My doctor ordered complete bed rest. At that time it was not possible for my husband to take time off from his job. My Birth to Three group pitched in to help. In addition to babysitting my daughter in their homes, they took turns providing us with an evening meal and even volunteered to clean the house! Quite frankly, I don't know how I could have managed without their help and caring."

a Birth to Three parent

"I live in a rural area. I worked before I had kids, then I quit to stay home—did I get lonely! I was bored and confused. . . . I called the Birth to Three office one day. The girl let me talk a long time, told me about a group starting up. That was two years ago, and we all still meet. I found others who were lonely and scared of motherhood—they let me cry and laugh about it, but best of all, they all said, 'Hey, yeah, *me too.*' I wasn't alone in my feelings of guilt about not always liking the role of mother. They've helped me control my actions when I'm angry, find other methods, think about my child's

way of thinking. Thanks for letting me put my 'two cents' worth in . . . you people saved my life."
a Birth to Three parent

"It helps to understand that I'm not the only parent that wonders if I'm going to make it through the day. Sometimes I feel at the end of my rope, like I can't take it any longer. Then I know I'm not the only one with those problems. I can call someone in my Birth to Three group, try other parents' ways of dealing with things. It helps to find out that others go through the same things and problems and they survive it."
a Birth to Three parent

"I have always left a Birth to Three meeting feeling encouraged and refreshed. This past year has been a particularly hard one for me, financial difficulties, separation from my husband, changes in living arrangements. And with all the turmoil, I've always found the Birth to Three group understanding, supportive, and loving. My problems seem to become more manageable when I'm able to share them."
a Birth to Three parent

"I feel so fortunate to have had Birth to Three. . . . Anytime I feel I've begun to repay this organization for all the comfort they've provided me, I receive more. . . . My brother and I were abused as children. Had there been a group such as Birth to Three 40 years ago, I believe my mother would have joined for the social contact and educational information she sought. I have to believe she would have been helped, and perhaps *stopped.*"
a Birth to Three parent, now a group leader

Statements from Professionals

"I am extremely supportive of the work of Birth to Three and am confident that our cooperative relationship will benefit even more children as you expand your services to include teenage parents. I look forward to continuing to explore other areas of collaboration between Birth to Three and 4J. Thank you for your dedication to our most vulnerable little ones. It matters!"

Margaret Nichols, Superintendent,
School District 4J

"Birth to Three is one of the few primary prevention services that has originated in this community in recent years. The early and continued success of the groups are proof that this kind of involvement is welcome and needed by young parents, particularly mothers. The organization has utilized volunteers and in every way tried to stretch their funds. I strongly recommend Birth to Three as a productive organization that any funding source could feel secure in which to invest their resources."

Ardie Arnis,
Chair, United Way Allocations Committee,
past Parent/Child Program Manager,
Lane Co. Health Division

"The mental health needs of our culture can never be adequately met through its conventional institutions. The need far exceeds the resource. What hope we do have, short of undergoing major cultural changes, is to develop innovative, preventative programs based on people helping people, programs that are community-based rather than institution-

12

based. . . . Birth to Three is a step in this direction."
Dr. Bruce Strimling, pediatrician

"Every community should have a parent support program like Birth to Three. It works like a loving grandmother, a circle of true friends, and a sympathetic information bureau. It's what all parents need. . . before, during, and for long after the birth of a baby, especially in these strained times, and in our tense society."
Dr. Benjamin Spock

"Birth to Three is a community investment of the most priceless kind: an investment in the preservation of nurturing family life which ought to be the birthright of every child."
Dave Frohnmayer
Oregon State Attorney General

"I want to wish you a hearty congratulations on the occasion of your fifth birthday (November, 1983). The benefits parents receive from Birth to Three, unlike others, will be passed down from our generation to each new generation of parents. Your efforts are truly like the waters of a small spring which evolve into a mighty, flowing river. I commend you on your ability to persevere, and for the human kindness and care Birth to Three provides to parents and their children. I am pleased to have been your project officer, I wish you the best of luck and continued success."
Roland Sneed,
Social Services Program Specialist,
National Center on
Child Abuse and Neglect

CHAPTER 1

Becoming a New Parent

Dealing with the everyday needs of infants and young children is an entirely new experience that is hard for a prospective parent to imagine. The largely romanticized images of parenthood portrayed by television, radio, and magazines complicate the situation by creating unrealistic expectations. Television mothers and fathers always seem to say the right things to their children and to each other, and the mistakes they do make lead to amusing and short-lived problems. Glossy magazine ads show fathers coming home from work to find unruffled mothers in tidy homes, cuddling their babies. These idyllic pictures suggest to new parents that they can anticipate an effortless glide through childrearing. Sometimes the transition to new parenthood seems blissfully easy. But often, such an idealization makes a difficult job even harder. It contributes to the needless anxiety and guilt that is common among parents who are caught up in the natural turbulence that accompanies a new baby. Mothers who compare their own imperfect reality with an ideal standard often find themselves haunted by unanswerable questions such as: "Have I bonded enough with the baby?"; "Has my C-section baby missed out on something?"; "Have I failed as a mother by choosing not to breastfeed?" Perhaps the most unsettling question is, "Do I really love this baby all the time?"

Many mothers, bewildered by their babies' crying, feel exhausted, overwhelmed, and on the verge of tears themselves. "I never knew it was going to be this way. My own mother didn't prepare me for this," the mother of a one-month-old infant complained in a Birth to Three group. For many new parents, coming home from the hospital is like falling into a void. The anticipation of childbirth is replaced by days and nights that run together, and endless chaos in the house.

Having a baby creates enormous changes in the lives of the parents. Caring for an infant means that personal needs and interests must be put aside. At least at the start, the usual pleasant activities, like stepping out for lunch with friends or going fishing for the weekend, are unthinkable. Career and housekeeping standards must be relaxed to make time for your partner and your baby. Assuming the role of parenthood also changes the way you think about yourself and the way you relate to your partner. It is hard, at the beginning, to keep up the old romance after becoming "Mom" and "Dad." The sense of humor that once came easily can be hard to summon when your life seems consumed by the baby. Many couples become tired and irritable, and begin to wonder what has happened to their relationship. There is less money and less time to spend together, and for awhile a sex life may seem like a thing of the past. These circumstances can make it difficult for the couple to work together and continue to nurture and support each other. Yet, this is a time when the original bond between the couple is more important than ever. Parents must learn to work together as a team to keep their relationship strong while providing for the needs of their growing infant. This is part of the challenge that is faced by new parents.

Social isolation greatly increases the difficulties experienced by parents. Many studies show that social contacts and support from others serve a vital function in maintaining the morale of mothers with young children. Positive social contacts help mitigate the stress of childrearing by providing an outlet for frustrations. Friends and relatives are a valuable resource if they live nearby and are willing to watch the baby or help with household chores. Unfortunately, many new parents find themselves without such support. If the family has just moved into the area, they might not have had time to develop close friendships. Even if the parents have good friends in the area, those friends may not have raised children.

While there is no doubt that the lives of both adults are changed by parenthood, it is the person caring for the baby, typically the mother, for whom the change is most complete. Caring for a new baby can be indescribably satisfying, but hard. New mothers often find their sense of time distorted by the apparently endless cycle of cleaning, washing, and feeding that can easily consume 10 or more hours of the day. At best, there may be periods of perhaps 30 minutes here or there in which to accomplish something, *anything,* before the baby awakens. Many women find the constant disorder in their homes disheartening, particularly if things had previously been neat and organized. Even if exhausted, a new mother may find it hard to rest while the baby sleeps—resting seems unproductive when there is so much to be done.

For a woman who worked before becoming a mother, balancing the demands of family life and a career is a challenge. These mothers must choose between earning a living and taking care of their babies full time. Returning to work is often essential because the extra money is needed more than ever to support the family. Continuing to work outside the home may also be necessary in order to achieve long-range career goals. For mothers who were previously employed, the physical and social isolation of being at home with a small baby can be particularly demoralizing. Perhaps for the first time, the new mother is spending many hours every day without adult companionship. Often, returning to work is considered important for maintaining self-esteem and helps women avoid feeling that they are stagnating. It also gives them something to talk about other than the mundane events and occasional high spots of domestic life. On the other hand, many women who had sworn confidently that they would return to work after the baby was born change their minds when they find they cannot bring themselves to leave the baby in someone else's care. Mothers who work part time may feel that their performance is inadequate both at home and at work. No matter what choice is made, many working women who become mothers feel torn about their decision regarding child care.

Sheila Kitzinger, in *Women as Mothers,* describes a self-conscious style of mothering which she suggests is typical of urban middle-class women. A mother who is intent on achieving a good relationship with her baby may find herself "so completely sucked into serving the infant's needs that she feels 'drained'. . . becomes resentful, as a result feels guilty, overcompensates by sacrificing herself still further. . . and then becomes more anxious and depressed" (pages 38-39). How many of us might recognize ourselves here? When speaking candidly, many mothers admit feeling inadequate and are convinced that other mothers cope better. In a typical expression of these feelings, one woman described her weekly Birth to Three meeting as "my pressure-release valve. What a relief it is to hear that I'm not the only one who feels this way, to know that I'm normal. Meeting this way makes me feel that what I'm doing as a mother is worthwhile."

An English journalist, writing on the value of female friendship, interviewed 40 married women living in London about their health. These women dedicated most of their time to child care and housework and had no paid work outside the home. She found a very high level of medically diagnosed depression among them; only 13 out of the 40 had *not* received tranquilizers or antidepressants at some stage in their lives as wives and mothers. For some of the women who were interviewed, the importance of female friendship was obvious—they reported that those times when they were friendless and isolated were much more bleak than when they had developed friendships with other women. One woman described it this way: "I feel a lot better since we got to know each other. It's terrible around here if you don't know anybody. You don't see anybody all day. It was like that all the time except for weekends when you had your husband." Some women spoke enthusiastically about the way in which friendships with other women eased personal worries and frequently became substitutes for visits to the doctor. Typically, the value of female friendship was linked very much to shared experience. "If I stopped seeing my friends I'd be back on the lonely trail, wouldn't I. . .back to the depression stage. I find that talking to my friends can be a lot easier than talking to my husband. Let's face it, he's a smashing bloke but he doesn't understand. He can't understand. He's at work all day so he doesn't know the situation. Where if you speak to these women they're more sympathetic. They're in the same boat as me. They've all got young children, they're at home, and if I feel a bit down about something I can talk to them about it and I find I feel a lot better" (Carol Paris, "The Guardian," August 7, 1981).

Stress and depression manifest themselves in symptoms such as irritability, constant tiredness, lowered self-esteem, and apathy. These symptoms are not only unpleasant in their own right, but they imperil the very social interactions upon which a mother depends. For example, as her own emotional state deteriorates, a mother is more likely to react irritably to her partner. This irritability makes it more difficult for her

19

partner to give her the support that she so desperately needs. In this light, it is hardly surprising that couple relationships are particularly vulnerable during the first few years after the birth of a baby.

Bad moods also interfere with the interactions between mother and child, with negative consequences for both. The mother becomes less effective in implementing her childrearing skills, which contributes to unpleasant behavior in her children. As the children become more disruptive, the mother's mood is eroded further, and her child-management skills continue to deteriorate. Some psychologists call this the "negativity cycle." At the very least, the mother's depressed state makes it difficult for her to enjoy being a parent. It also deprives the child of the high-quality interactions needed for cognitive and emotional development.

Becoming a parent is a "normal" life crisis that most of us undergo which involves vast psychological changes. Some parents are more able to cope with the changes than others. Unfortunately, until their need becomes extreme, there are few organized services available for those parents who do need help. By relying on the resources of parents themselves, informal peer-support networks can help to fill the gap left by social service programs. A postpartum support network such as Birth to Three can provide for the needs of new parents in three ways: 1) it reduces the isolation of new parents by providing them with social support from others also experiencing the transition to parenthood; 2) it offers an opportunity to discuss a broad range of concerns and family issues with others in similar circumstances; and 3) with the help of trained leaders and outside speakers, it offers education for parenthood at a formative period in the development of the family. Furthermore, a support network lacks the stigma often attached to a social service agency. Certainly everyone has problems, but not everyone (because of financial reasons, stereotypes, or ideologies) is willing to take those problems to mental health professionals. Many of us would rather talk to people in more natural contexts, to friends, family, and people who are in the same situation.

Under normal conditions, most parents find that raising children has both joys and aggravations. The "secret" to good parenting is keeping the difficulties to a minimum and putting them in perspective. Sharing the experience with other people (especially other parents) helps achieve both objectives, by providing information and support. Moreover, it provides them in a uniquely effective way. Although it deals with problem solving, Birth to Three is not primarily problem oriented. Rather, it is a good way to meet other people in the neighborhood who have small children; it provides a place to go where a baby is welcome, and offers an opportunity for fun and stimulation. At the same time, the groups help parents see one another through the rough spells that all parents face, however much they know.

CHAPTER 2

The Birth to Three Perspective

Many of the issues involved in raising a child from birth to three years of age affect all parents, regardless of their economic, political, or social situations. Birth to Three was organized with this commonality in mind. The program has been designed to provide information and support to parents with diverse personal philosophies and lifestyles. For this reason Birth to Three does not take a position on controversial issues such as career *vs.* full-time parenting, breast *vs.* bottle feeding, and right-to-life *vs.* right-to-choice. One particular approach to childrearing is not advocated over another, and there is no pressure on individuals to change their basic beliefs. As a result, Birth to Three is uniquely able to reach out to a wide segment of new parents and bring them together. We believe that parenting is an extremely important undertaking; our goal is simply to promote good parenting skills and positive attitudes toward childrearing that are consistent with the parents' philosophy.

The value of bringing parents with diverse backgrounds together became evident during our early attempts to organize specialized groups for parents. When Birth to Three was in the planning stage, we considered organizing support groups according to whether or not the mothers were college educated, breastfeeding, had a home birth, were living with the father of their baby, and so on. We thought that the participants would be more compatible and the discussion more lively if we formed groups of people with similar attitudes. However, after some deliberation we realized that matching people up this way would be difficult and time-consuming. Moreover, it would force us to begin our relationship with parents by asking them personal questions which intruded on their privacy. Organizing groups along neighborhood lines was much easier and made it possible for parents to see each other more regularly. In fact, we have found that groups composed of parents with diverse backgrounds are much more interesting. Parenthood has been called a great leveler, creating a common experience for people whose lives are otherwise very different. Indeed, discovering this common ground is an enriching experience for most people. In most groups, it soon becomes apparent that the different participants have complementary skills and strengths.

When parents have special problems, we have found that it is usually more effective to "mainstream" them into ordinary groups whenever possible, rather than isolate them in specialized groups. Joining a group for parents with babies that have developmental disorders, for instance, might cause participants to feel stigmatized; in such a group the members might feel obligated to focus on their babies' problems. In contrast, when two or three mothers of infants with special problems are part of a regular group, everyone has an opportunity to understand the needs of exceptional children and the demands that they place on their caretakers. Many of the experiences of mothers with normal children are pertinent to mothers with exceptional children. Many babies, exceptional or not, have feeding difficulties or impossible sleeping habits that can put a strain on siblings and marriages. Hearing other parents' stories may show mothers of infants with special needs that they are coping better than they thought. In some cases, however, we have found that parents in special circumstances are more comfortable talking about their situation with others who are peers. We have established groups for teenage mothers, single parents, and parents who were abused as children in response to requests for these types of support groups. The choice is always left up to the parents; they can join an ordinary group, a special group, or be a member of both.

Another valuable outcome of heterogeneous grouping is that extreme viewpoints tend to be moderated by other people's experience. For example, after hearing a woman tell about how she was unable to breastfeed her cleft palate baby, it would be unlikely for anyone to advance the claim that breastfeeding is "the only way," or that breastfeeding produces superior children. It is the group leader's job to maintain a balanced discussion and create an atmosphere in which no one is made to feel threatened by another's views or comments. This can be accomplished by presenting a variety of sources of information, often with the help of an invited speaker, and by encouraging everyone to express his or her opinion. Throughout, it is important for the group leader to show respect for the viewpoints that are offered and to prevent anyone from dominating the discussion. This approach allows group members to sort out the facts for themselves and form their own opinions.

Birth to Three is a nonstigmatizing and nonjudgmental vehicle for bringing new parents of all persuasions together. It creates a comfortable setting in which people can share their thoughts and choose their own level of participation. No one feels pressured to compete or convince others that she or he is a perfect mother or father. Most parents are relieved when they discover that negative feelings, tensions, and ambivalence are experienced by other parents. A sense of humor about things often comes more easily within the context of a group and can help to defuse situations that otherwise look unbearable.

Because the demands of parenting are an all-day, every-day affair, it is important that parents have support systems composed of other parents, not professionals. Birth to Three groups are usually set up by a staff member or volunteer with some training in child development and counseling. However, she is a peer to the other mothers and portrays herself as such. Her expertise is seen as coming from personal experience with small children of her own. In our society, relatively few people make use of the services provided by mental health professionals. When people need help they usually seek advice from a friend, a relative, or a neighbor who is a well-trusted listener. Seeing a professional for therapy can be both expensive and stigmatizing. This is particularly true for low-income families who cannot afford (and may not trust) the largely middle-class mental health establishment. Birth to Three is appealing to many parents because it is not directly connected with mental health or medical establishments. It is purely an organization of parents.

Birth to Three support groups complement professional pediatric care. We do not attempt to be a source of medical opinion or advice. Medical questions that arise during "warm line" telephone calls and group meetings are always referred to the medical community. Still, there are many matters that do not require consultation with a doctor, and many pediatricians would be relieved to have less of their time taken up with those very real but not necessarily medically significant issues. Colic is one, routine toilet training is another. Many parents feel awkward about calling their doctor "just" for reassurance. On those difficult days when it would be nice to be

26

airlifted out of the house, few mothers feel comfortable about calling their pediatrician to talk. A conversation with another mother would be more helpful.

Birth to Three groups function as a sort of extended family setting from which new parents can draw support into their relationships with each other and their babies. Support comes from other parents as well as from the leader. We feel that parents whose own needs are being met are more effective in attending to the needs of their children. In our view, concentrating services on parents helps them feel better about themselves, encourages a positive orientation to childrearing, reduces frustration and child abuse, and works to prevent problems in the parents' relationship with one another—all in the best interests of the baby.

CHAPTER 3

The Beginnings of Birth to Three

The Author as a New Parent

When our first child was born my husband and I received an odd, but perhaps appropriate, gift from friends who did not have children. It was a poster, an enlargement of a drawing from *Alice's Adventures in Wonderland,* in which Alice holds a baby pig that she has just rescued from the rampaging Duchess. The caption underneath read, "Now, what am I going to do with this creature when I get it home?"

Even during the worst moments I never wondered whether our baby might metamorphize into a pig. On the other hand, after I brought the baby home I had only the vaguest idea about what to do next. During my pregnancy, like many parents, I read and reread all the books I could lay my hands on. These were mostly about pregnancy, diet, exercise, and delivery. Regarding life beyond delivery, I had read very little. Indeed, I had no firsthand experience with infants, although I did know some two-year-olds. My mother lived thousands of

miles away, as did my mother-in-law, and, although enthusiastic, neither could offer much practical help. Within minutes after coming home from the hospital, the baby began to
cry and kept crying more or less steadily for the next few
weeks. Perhaps to an experienced parent it would have been
obvious that this was a clear case of colic. I remember a sym-

pathetic neighbor showing us how to rock the crib to induce sleep. We learned other strategies with time, but on the whole that first period was rough. Frankly, I was intimidated by the baby for months, and so thoroughly exhausted that I was ready to fall asleep whenever the opportunity came along. Reading put me to sleep almost instantly, and once I dozed off in the bathtub.

When our second child was born a few years later, I felt quite capable of taking on another baby. I had been through this once before and I knew how it was done. The first half year or so was a definite improvement over the first time. However, when our baby was around six months old, it occurred to me that I knew no one else with an infant. Moreover, I knew very few people who stayed home during the day with small children. My street seemed to empty itself of cars in the early morning and my forays around the neighborhood produced no adult companionship. One day, while shopping in a department store, I noticed a woman in the aisle near me. I took a few moments to study her—she was holding a baby about the same size as mine and she looked pleasant enough, so I went over and asked how old her baby was. We went through sleeping habits, feeding problems, bad tempers, and the rest. After a few minutes, I knew that I had found someone who could be a friend. But there had to be a better way to meet people.

How Birth to Three Was Started

Birth to Three was started by three women in Eugene, Oregon. Minalee Saks, Sue Kelly and I were brought together by a research project on infant temperament at the University of Oregon. Sue and I were part of the research project staff and Minalee was a participant in the study. About 55 families with newborn infants took part. For 12 months the research staff made regular visits to the participants' homes and observed the babies interacting with their mothers. Most of the

31

mothers in the study regularly asked how the other babies were doing, how the other mothers felt about this or that, and whether various things were "normal." It occurred to us that many of these mothers might want to get together informally to discuss their experiences. When we tried to gauge interest in the idea of a support or discussion group by calling a first meeting, over half of the participants in the study showed up.

Although the response to that first meeting was very encouraging, none of us had the time to pursue the idea of starting a parent support network until almost a year later. By then we were no longer involved in the temperament study and we were all interested in starting something new. Among us, we had graduate training in nursing, teaching, and child development. All three of us were also mothers: Minalee and I had small babies, while Sue had five grown children. We were eager to do something that would combine our professional interests with our personal experience as parents.

Our first step was to investigate the services that were already available in the local community. The Eugene-Springfield area has a population of about 170,000. Both towns rely heavily on commerce and the timber industry. Eugene is also the home of the University of Oregon. We found that Lamaze and other childbirth education classes were offered for prospective parents, and many parents of three-year-olds could meet each other through their children's nursery schools. But there were very few services designed to help parents with babies contact one another. The La Leche League did offer classes and a very fine telephone counseling service. However, these services were available only to breastfeeding mothers. The only other options available for new parents were a postpartum support group for women whose infants had been born at home, and a series of parent-education classes offered by the local health department. These programs were well organized and thoughtful, but they addressed specific needs and were available only to a limited number of new parents.

Since then, we have found that this is a common situation in many communities. Typically, there are some programs for children and parents with special needs and interests; for example, there are programs for children with learning disabilities, speech and language problems, or diseases such as diabetes. There may also be programs for abusive parents and single parents. Parents with school-aged children can often find classes such as Parent Effectiveness Training if they want to learn a particular orientation to discipline and communication. These are all important programs. However, the more specialized approaches to parent education are best suited to those parents who understand and endorse the philosophy of the particular program. Our goal was to design a program that would be open to all parents, regardless of their situation or beliefs. We wanted to use the parents themselves as a resource; by bringing parents together they could provide information and support for one another. Rather than replacing or competing with existing services, we hoped to place these services within a larger context that would encompass the needs of all parents.

There were many details to be worked out before the program could be put into operation. In the beginning, much of our time was spent reading, gathering information, and refining our ideas. The three of us met weekly (sometimes more often) in one another's homes, and talked almost daily on the telephone about the program as it began to take shape. We also consulted with various members of the community: parents, midwives, a pediatrician, a lawyer, psychologists, public health nurses, educators, counselors, and city administrators. As the program developed, we began to contact prospective parents. We asked a women's medical clinic to circulate copies of a questionnaire that asked women whether they found the idea of a postnatal support group appealing. Would they come to meetings? What would they like to talk about? Several dozen women responded, and almost all of them asked to be invited to the first meeting.

Although the response to our questionnaire suggested that we could start organizing groups immediately, we decided to wait until financial support could be arranged for the program. We realized that running a full-blown organization would require a level of effort that could only be sustained with a core group of paid staff members. We also felt that a source of funding would help us to achieve a higher standard of professionalism and increase public recognition of the value of our work. Even an organization that was staffed completely by volunteers would need some financing to pay the costs of running an office and setting up groups. At first we were opposed to asking parents to pay fees because we thought this would discourage many potential members. We also felt that peer support is something that should be offered without charge. It soon became apparent, however, that we would have to charge members a modest fee in order to make the program more self-sufficient. We approached various local organizations (the community college, the county public health department, and a family counseling agency) hoping to ally ourselves with one of them in order to boost our credibility locally and secure some financial backing. Although many of the people we contacted were encouraging and enthusiastic, there were no organizations financially able to take us in.

After reviewing our situation, we began to question whether we wanted to be absorbed into a large bureaucratic structure. Under those circumstances, we might lose control of our own program. On the other hand, if we formed our own private, nonprofit corporation, we could apply for grants ourselves. With the help of an attorney we completed the necessary forms and drew up a set of bylaws and personnel policies. For our board of directors we enlisted seven people who had been particularly encouraging and helpful.

After forming our nonprofit corporation, we continued to

explore funding possibilities. We applied to several Oregon foundations for grants and studied *The Federal Register* for relevant requests for proposals. Several astute grant writers at the University of Oregon coached us on the procedures for asking foundations for money. We interviewed the directors of several small nonprofit community service organizations in order to learn how they were structured and funded. We also met regularly with a group of public health nurses who regarded our plan as an important complement to their own programs. All of these people made an important contribution in helping us to think through our ideas, warning us about possible problems and suggesting fundraising strategies.

The next step was to take care of a few basic housekeeping matters. We decided on the name "Birth to Three" because it provided the best description of our target population. We considered "Parents' Resources" but felt that it was too vague. Various cute names were discarded, as were names that emphasized mothers and excluded fathers. We considered "Birth to Two" until a pediatrician reminded us that the year between two and three can often be very difficult. With this in mind, we designed the program to include parents through their child's third year (we now find that some groups continue to meet on their own until their children are in kindergarten or beyond). A cheerful, child-oriented logo was created by Minalee's husband. We thought it best to steer away from logos that featured mothers and/or fathers with their children in order to avoid stereotypes; this also eliminated the possibility of any racial, class, or ethnic overtones that might be associated with the depiction of human figures.

A telephone listing with an accompanying entry in the yellow pages under the Social Services heading was another necessity for Birth to Three. At first, the telephone was located in my home and, later, in Sue's. We agreed that we would try working out of our homes, in order to save money and make us more available to our families. Although this arrangement had definite advantages, the drawbacks soon became apparent. As Birth to Three became better known in the community, the telephone rang incessantly and the paper clutter in our kitchens and bedrooms became overwhelming. We eventually decided to move the telephone and most of the clutter to an office that was donated by a local mental health organization.

About midway through this planning year we responded to a request for proposals from the United States Department of Health, Education, and Welfare (now the Department of Health and Human Services). Together with Family Services (a nonprofit family counseling agency in Eugene), we submitted a proposal to offer the following services:

Neighborhood Groups organized to put new parents in contact with one another and provide a source for new friends, ideas, and mutual support. Groups were to be formed for mothers, fathers, couples, teenage parents, and single parents.

Peer Counseling available by telephone or home visits for parents experiencing stress, needing information on child development, or just wanting to talk to someone. Parents could also telephone Birth to Three for information about services available elsewhere in the community and for appropriate referrals.

A Community Resource Poster given to parents as they left the hospital with their new baby. This poster was to contain the names and telephone numbers of local agencies serving parents' needs, a bibliography of books available at the local library, and a description of Birth to Three services.

A Monthly Newsletter that contained notices of relevant community events, book reviews, research excerpts, feature articles, and contributions from parents.

Meetings and Workshops scheduled monthly featuring

speakers, films, book discussions, and other educational events.

Low-cost professional counseling was also to be provided by Family Services for parents who needed more than peer support. Family Services would accept referrals, especially where stress was high, from physicians and from other organizations in the community as well as from Birth to Three; parents in the community would also be encouraged to come in directly for help. Family Services could also refer parents to Birth to Three for continued support. Through a Homemaker Program, Family Services would send a person trained in "home economics" skills into the home to relieve a parent who was ill or emotionally exhausted and had no other resources for help. This service would be offered to parents at a very low cost.

After several months, we were notified that the proposal was accepted and funding would start in October, 1978. By this time, Sue had left Eugene with her family to spend a sabbatical year in Europe. She rejoined us a year later, but meanwhile Minalee and I hired two additional staff members. Each of us worked half time; one person edited the newsletter and the others put their efforts into organizing groups and managing the other parts of the program. As the program grew, we began to train volunteers to lead the groups that we had started. It then became necessary to assign the job of volunteer coordinator to a staff member who assumed primary responsibility for recruiting, training, and supervising volunteers to lead groups.

It soon became apparent that managing Birth to Three was going to be more than a half-time undertaking. Originally, we tried to limit ourselves to organizing groups in the three areas of Eugene and Springfield where the largest number of babies were concentrated. However, the program grew much faster than we had ever anticipated. As novices with a good idea, we had failed to realize how popular the program would be and how much effort it would take to manage an organization that had grown so large. In addition, the conditions of our HEW grant forced us to spend increasing amounts of time on fundraising. The grant provided 100% of our original budget during the first year, 80% during the second year, and 50% during the third. After that, we were on our own. In order to receive HEW funds for the second and third years, we had to come up with the remaining portion of our budget. This meant that we had to start raising those additional funds immediately. We spent enormous amounts of time organizing fundraising activities, searching out foundations, writing proposals, and making presentations to local groups. Fortunately, our efforts were successful. In retrospect, it is easy to see that these activities are an important part of making an organization better known in the community, but the time required for fundraising certainly hadn't been anticipated when we created our "half-time" jobs.

A second demand that we had not anticipated was the time needed for correspondence, report writing, and record keeping. Although these administrative jobs might have been done most efficiently by one person, we divided the administrative work among us, since each of us wanted to spend at least part of our time working with parents. We also felt it was important for the entire staff to be involved in program planning and organizational decision making. As a result, we became a tightly knit staff that spent a lot of time in staff meetings. In the last few years as our program and staff have expanded and evolved, each staff member's duties have become much more circumscribed. For example, we now have one staff person who takes care of managing grants, one program administrator, and one volunteer coordinator.

Although our enthusiasm for the program remains as strong as ever, we've found it necessary to set limits on our work commitments in order to do our jobs effectively and not become overwhelmed. For several years, the telephones in our homes would ring all day and we would feel obligated to spend long periods on the phone with a parent who felt pushed to the limit while our own children howled. Burnout threatened constantly. In retrospect, some of those herculean efforts were necessary while we developed the program. We endured together with a mixture of good faith and strong interpersonal relations, but we could not have sustained the pace for very long. The future of the program and our own mental health demanded that we organize ourselves a little better, set some goals aside temporarily, and persuade each other not to work full time at a supposedly part-time undertaking. We believe that our experiences have produced a coherent program that you can adopt without having to make the same mistakes. The following chapters describe in detail the steps for setting up Birth to Three style programs, with an emphasis on how you can modify our general program to suit your specific circumstances.

CHAPTER 4

Organizing and Running Parent Support Groups

Birth to Three's purpose is straightforward: bring parents together so they can share information and give support to one another. The concept is flexible enough to be applied in many different ways. Successful programs can range from a single mother organizing occasional meetings for a group of friends to a health or mental health professional setting up a network of groups throughout a community. In fact, our own program progressed from several demonstration groups to a regional network. This chapter provides step-by-step guidelines for setting up a program that is suited to your particular circumstances. By encouraging other people to become involved in our program and draw upon our experience, we hope that Birth to Three groups will become established nationwide. New parent support programs *should* be available to families in every community.

As new groups are formed across the country, we would like to encourage them to become part of the Birth to Three

41

network by registering as an affiliated group or organization. For information on costs and procedures, write to: Registration Coordinator, Birth to Three, 3411-1 Willamette St., Eugene, OR 97405 (please be sure to enclose a self-addressed stamped envelope for our reply). Comprehensive materials for training volunteers to be group facilitators (including curricula for working with parents of toddlers, teenage parents, and parents under stress), sample grant proposals, information on setting up babysitting cooperatives, and many other useful resources have been developed and are available at a reasonable cost. Write for our free list of "Birth to Three Supplementary Materials." We feel strongly that there is a place for organizations like Birth to Three in every community and we're eager to help in any way that we can.

Three Working Models for Birth to Three Programs

This section describes three possible models for providing Birth to Three programs to new parents in your community: running informal groups; organizing several groups; and setting up community-wide programs. Each working model represents a different level of commitment and organizational structure. Because there are many different ways to organize and run parent support programs that are equally valid, readers are encouraged to think of these models as a place to start in designing their own program.

Informal Groups

A group of new parents does not have to be large or elaborate to be worthwhile. For many parents, the easiest "group" to put together would be made up of people they already know—friends, acquaintances, and neighbors. Even three or four mothers would be enough for a small group. This type of informal group could meet at the home of one of the members and discuss whatever topics the group chooses. It is usually best to schedule topics in advance (with the understanding that the scheduled topics can be superseded by more pressing issues). This prevents the conversation from wandering and gives the group a sense of progress. The eight discussion outlines presented in Chapter 7 provide a survey of issues that are important to new parents and guidelines for leading meetings on specific topics. The Birth to Three newsletter is another good source of material for group discussion. The newsletter is written in a style that is jargon-free and easy-to-read so that the articles can be enjoyed by any parent. Reading about the experiences of other parents and other groups in the newsletter will help you to improve your program and creates a sense of belonging to a larger network. One possibility is to schedule some of the group meetings around the arrival of each newsletter; this will ensure that the group meets on a regular basis and that there are some well-defined topics to talk about. No matter how you choose topics for discussion, it is important to be organized. Try to make it a policy to decide at each meeting what the topics will be for the next meeting and assign any readings or "homework" that the members of the group should complete. Many groups set up a quarterly "planning meeting" to agree on topics and activities for the next few months. A calendar of upcoming meetings is then drawn up and given to everyone.

Even an informal group can provide additional services for its members and the community. For example, members could help one another with babysitting needs or provide the nucleus for a babysitting co-op. If group members committed themselves to watching one another's children during one evening every other week it would be possible for everyone to have an occasional night out. A small group could also research the services that are available to new parents in the community or compile a list of nursery schools and other child-care facilities in the area.

You may find after meeting in a small group that it would

be stimulating to have some new parents join the group. In that case, the section that follows on "recruiting parents" is pertinent. New members bring with them additional information and perspectives, and can ensure the group's survival if its founders move away or find themselves unable to attend meetings.

Organizing Several Groups

A more ambitious application of the Birth to Three model would be to organize a small network of three or four groups that share resources. This could be accomplished by one or two energetic new parents, or by a parent who has been involved in a Birth to Three group and whose children are now a little older. The Birth to Three concept has also been successfully incorporated into ongoing mental health programs by social services professionals. Typically, these programs are designed to address the needs of "at-risk" parents such as single parents, teenage parents, and parents with a history of child abuse. Health and mental health agencies may also find it within the scope of their outreach services to offer support groups for parents in generally easier circumstances.

One distinct advantage of more ambitious programs is that they can provide more services and thus have a greater impact on the immediate community. As a program gains visibility and popularity, it is easier to find new members for additional groups. In fact, you may find that the services offered by your program are so much in demand that several groups will quickly grow out of the first group that you start. The full range of services that structured local groups or networks can offer includes arranging for speakers, producing a community resources poster, and offering peer counseling (these are described in detail in Chapter 5).

When a group is not made up of friends and neighbors, a strategy is needed for recruiting new members. An effective and inexpensive method is to put up notices at bus stops, li-

44

braries, clinics, stores, and other places that parents frequent. The notice should extend an invitation to a first meeting at a particular time and place, and give the name and telephone number of someone to call for more information. A "generic" flier that can be photocopied and filled in for this purpose appears in Appendix 4.1. Often, local pediatricians will give your name and telephone number to parents who might be interested. It is also a good idea to make use of television and radio stations that broadcast public service announcements free of charge. Similar publicity can be arranged by contacting the local newspaper. Our own procedure for contacting parents is described in the next section of this chapter; although very successful, it requires a considerable amount of staff or volunteer time.

The first meeting might be in someone's home or in a public meeting room. The goal for this meeting is to get acquainted with one another and decide where the group will meet and how regularly. Some basic organizational decisions should be made, including choosing one or two members to facilitate the discussion at the next meeting. The discussions themselves can be organized around the material presented in Chapter 7. Planning group discussions and activities together gives everyone an idea of what to expect at meetings as well as the feeling that each person's contribution is important. If too many people show up at the first meeting, the group can be divided into several smaller units that are organized according to neighborhoods or children's ages.

Setting Up Community-wide Programs

The ultimate application of the Birth to Three model is to set up a comprehensive, community-wide program. Perhaps the best example of an extensive program is provided by the Birth to Three organization in the Eugene-Springfield area. Each year approximately 3200 new parents receive Birth to Three's community resources poster when they leave the hos-

45

pital with their newborn baby. Between seven and eight hundred parents participate in groups and classes each year. Approximately 500 parents attend regularly scheduled educational events, and about 1200 parents call our peer-counseling "warm line" every year to talk about problems they are having. It is estimated that a total of 10,000 peer-counseling calls are made by group leaders to members of their groups each year. Over 1100 families receive our bimonthly newsletter which features book reviews, interviews, stories written by Birth to Three members, articles on child development, and information about relevant local events. In addition to offering support groups and classes in the Eugene-Springfield area, Birth to Three also organizes support groups for parents living in rural areas in the county. Special groups have been formed for adolescent parents, and a series of lecture-discussion meetings has been arranged for parents under stress, including parents who are single, unemployed, low-income, or who were themselves abused as children. All of this is accomplished with the equivalent of four full-time staff positions that are shared by seven women. This kind of outreach is possible only through the extensive use of over 100 trained volunteers, most of whom are graduates of Birth to Three groups. With proper training and supervision, these parents are uniquely qualified to help other parents.

Laying the Groundwork. Before even a simple network can be started, a certain amount of "homework" needs to be done. The first step is to assess the needs and resources of your community so that your Birth to Three organization can be designed to complement existing services. The second step is to evaluate your skills and those of your "staff" so that decisions can be made concerning the responsibilities of each person and the range of services that you will be able to offer. The third step is to think carefully about the type of organizational structure you will need in order to achieve your goals. It is important to work through each of these steps before you begin setting up your program—the ultimate success of your organization will depend, in many ways, upon the decisions that are made in the beginning.

Your first assignment is to learn about the services that are already available in the community. Talk to people you know, parents and professionals in the medical and mental health fields, officials in local government, and professors at the local university or community college. In particular, ask them about the gaps that exist in the local educational and social services system. Talking with professionals in the community about your project establishes you as a credible entity and helps to refine your ideas. In addition to seeking out public officials, also consult some of the parents who are likely to use the services that you are thinking about offering. Discussions with parents will give you some idea about the types of people who might get involved in your organization; this feedback is an important factor in developing a service that will meet their needs. Because of the contacts, information, and credibility that it can bring, there is no substitute for this advance work.

Staff Development. At this point, you should have a small group of people who have expressed interest in helping to set up a Birth to Three program in your community. With luck, you have also found some professionals who support your efforts and will provide referrals to your organization. The next step is to consider the skills of each staff member and divide the anticipated job responsibilities accordingly. The initial tasks will include recruiting members, leading the first group meetings, and handling administrative details such as keeping a list of members, coordinating staff activities, and fundraising.

You will have to decide if you are going to pay yourselves a salary. An organization with a paid staff is likely to accomplish more than one that is run by volunteers. Office work requires a kind of continuity and intensity that is best suited to salaried staff. Providing at least part-time salaries for a core group of staff members will not only make your program much more effective but will add to its credibility in the eyes of the community. Moreover, helping parents is professional work worthy of pay. The reality, however, is that money is hard to raise and staff salaries can easily become the largest item in your budget. A more realistic plan may be to rely heavily on volunteer help in the beginning stages of your organization with the goal of generating enough money to pay salaries when your organization becomes more established.

This is a good time to estimate how much money you will need and how to raise it. Try to anticipate the expenses involved in running your proposed program and draw up a budget. Consider the idea of charging membership fees and review the other fundraising ideas that are presented in Chapter 6. Put together a contingency budget in case you are not able to raise the money you need; decide in advance where you will trim your budget if necessary. This helps workers plan for the future and makes fundraisers aware of the programs that are threatened if their efforts are unsuccessful.

Choosing an Organizational Structure. There are two basic issues involved in selecting an appropriate organizational structure for your program: how decisions are to be made, and whether or not to become a nonprofit corporation. The subject of how decisions are made will undoubtedly arise as you work out staff positions and responsibilities. It is very important to discuss this thoroughly before your program begins. One possibility is to create a "horizontal" organization in which the responsibility for designing the program and making policy decisions is shared among the staff. A "vertical" organization with recognized lines of authority and a "director" is another possibility. Each arrangement has its strengths and weaknesses. For example, decisions are made more quickly in a vertical structure, while a horizontal structure is more democratic and results in decisions that reflect the consensus of the group. Horizontal organizations create a feeling of togetherness and commitment, yet they can fall apart when personal conflicts or serious policy disagreements arise.

As your organization expands, you may find that the structure designed for a small group no longer meets your needs. A larger staff and more elaborate programs usually require individuals to take on more specialized roles. The people who contact your organization will also need to know who is responsible for what. For example, institutional sponsors will expect a larger organization to have a secretary, personnel director, advertising manager, and so on. In a horizontal organization you may still need to assign these titles to staff members to keep outsiders from being confused, but those positions need not be given the status that similar positions receive in a vertical organization. One strategy is to begin with a horizontal structure and then gradually shift to a more vertical structure when your program is in full swing. Some of the benefits of a horizontal structure could also be preserved within a vertical structure by rotating key roles and keeping salaries equal.

Another major decision has to do with whether or not to incorporate as a nonprofit organization and apply for tax-exempt status. There are several advantages to setting up a nonprofit structure like the one we have in Eugene. Most importantly, it allows your organization to make use of public and private sources of funding that are otherwise not available. If you intend to write grants and approach institutions such as foundations and government agencies, then nonprofit status is a must. A nonprofit organization can also accept donations and generate support from fundraising drives. There are additional cost-saving benefits including cheaper mailing rates and discounts on purchases. On the other hand, running a formal nonprofit organization can be quite a burden on a small group of volunteers. An alternative approach is to incorporate the Birth to Three concept into an existing mental health, corporate, or social service organization. Setting up a network under an existing structure definitely simplifies many administrative tasks. However, it also means introducing a substantial change into an institution that may be inflexible or unaccustomed to dealing with the needs of new parents using a self-help model. If you are in doubt, discuss the different alternatives with the administrators of a few nonprofit organizations in your community; they are generally well informed and willing to help. You may want to consult an attorney to make sure that you are choosing the right structure. A good attorney can also help you file for incorporation, seek tax-exempt status, and establish a set of bylaws and personnel policies. An attorney makes an excellent board member because of the specialized help that he or she can provide in getting you off to a good start and keeping you on track.

Many of the new groups and community-wide programs will be put together by highly motivated parents with some time and skills to give to a worthwhile cause. Programs created in this fashion will probably begin on a smaller scale and find themselves retracing many of Birth to Three's steps as they grow. Programs with greater resources may attempt to offer a comprehensive set of services from the beginning. The framework you choose will obviously depend upon your resources and the community that you live in. No matter what institutional framework is adopted, it is the commitment of parents to improving their childrearing skills that makes Birth to Three support groups work.

Starting Parent Groups

Selecting Target Areas

When we began our program in the fall of 1978 we tried to maximize our impact by organizing groups in well-defined target areas. We selected two target areas in Eugene and one in Springfield on the basis of census tract reports that indicated these areas had the highest birth rates in the community.

50

Census information can be obtained from the public library or city planning office. Each tract is essentially a neighborhood "cluster" that can be covered in less than ten minutes by car. Grouping parents in this way enables members to get to meetings easily and to help each other with transportation, and makes it convenient for group members to get together between meetings. Individual staff members are responsible for organizing and running groups in each of the target areas. The concept of target areas does not, however, apply to the other services that are offered by our program. The newsletter, telephone peer counseling, community resources poster, and educational events are available to the entire community.

As more people hear about the program, parents living outside the target areas may call in and ask to join groups. If the groups are not already filled, our policy has been to try to include anyone who is interested in the program in a group. Parents who call in or are referred from outside the target areas are usually invited to join existing groups that are looking for new members. Parents who are having problems are always given priority regardless of where they live.

Recruiting Parents

Perhaps the easiest way to contact new parents is through hospital staff and pediatricians. Our experience has been that these professionals are very receptive to our program because it complements their own efforts to help parents and children. With the cooperation of the local medical establishment, all new parents receive a Birth to Three poster as they leave the hospital with their baby. This ensures that new parents are at least aware that a program such as Birth to Three is available to them. After receiving a poster many parents call the Birth to Three office and ask to join a group in their area.

Other parents, however, need some further contact before they decide to join, typically because they are uncomfortable with the idea of calling an office. Since hospitals and doctors cannot give out the names of their patients, the most efficient system that we have found to identify families with babies is to follow the daily birth announcements in the local newspaper. Most births are listed in the newspaper along with the address for each family. These are then plotted on a census tract map of the area (available from the City Manager's office) and a street guide that can be obtained through the post office. This job is now the responsibility of a volunteer who assembles a list every month of the 60 to 90 new families that need to be contacted. Each family is then sent a letter providing a second introduction to the services offered by Birth to Three (a sample letter appears in Appendix 4.2). The tone of the letter is low key, jargon-free, and friendly without being pushy. It ends by promising that someone from the Birth to Three office will call the parent in a few days with an invitation to join the group. About 20 to 25 letters are usually necessary to generate enough response to form a group of 10 parents. Before mailing out the letters, the group leader checks to make sure that each of the families has a listed telephone number. If a family does not, the group leader adds her telephone number and a note to the bottom of the letter inviting the family to contact her at home or at the Birth to Three office.

The Initial Telephone Call

Five or six days after the letter is mailed, the group leader calls each family and invites the parent(s) to attend a Birth to Three meeting that will be held the following week in their neighborhood. After providing information about the time and place of the meeting, the group leader asks if the parent(s) would like to come to the meeting with their baby. Although mothers are typically more active than fathers in our program, this initial invitation is extended to either parent who answers the phone. Usually the father will pass the telephone to the mother; sometimes, however, the father is the baby's primary caretaker or is equally interested in the program. Once, for example, we encountered a family in which both parents were teachers and the father stayed home to care for an infant and a three-year-old. This father, who joined a Birth to Three group, strongly resented telephone callers who assumed that he must be "looking after the kids for a few minutes while the mother was off shopping." His complaint emphasized for us the danger in casually assuming anything about a family's organization or attitudes. Couples' groups have become increasingly popular, and many Birth to Three groups plan regular evening meetings that alternate with daytime meetings so that fathers can attend.

To break the ice during these telephone calls, it usually helps to ask questions about how the parents and their baby are doing. How are the parents feeling? Are they getting enough rest? If there are any siblings, what do they think of the baby? The purpose of this first call is to offer some background information on Birth to Three, describe the services that are offered by the program, give the parents details about other community services that might be useful, and listen to the parents' concerns. We always begin the telephone call by asking if this is a good time to talk: "Are you busy right now? If you'd like, I could call you back later, at a more convenient time...."

When we started the program it was not easy to make these telephone calls—at times we felt as though we were selling something. Eventually we realized that most parents appreciate being contacted. In the pandemonium that usually accompanies the arrival of a new baby, some parents only vaguely remember bringing the Birth to Three poster home from the hospital and others have not had a chance to open the letter. Now that the program is well known, calling new parents is much easier. Indeed, within a year after starting our program, people were anticipating our telephone calls. Now many parents respond by saying, "I have friends who are in

Birth to Three groups and they've been telling me what it's like. When is the first meeting?"

Eight to 10 parents with babies is about the largest number of people that can be accommodated comfortably at a meeting. If the group leader calls 20 families, usually between 10 and 12 parents say they will come to the meeting and eight to 10 actually show up. Last minute changes in plans, tiredness, or illness make it hard for parents to make firm commitments. Most of the parents who come to the first meeting end up coming to subsequent meetings. Although two or three parents may drop out, new people usually take their places— someone may invite a friend, a parent from outside the target area may be directed to the group, or a parent who wasn't interested when the group was formed might decide to join a few months later. Groups generally stabilize at about 12 members, with eight in attendance at a typical meeting.

Recruiting parents with letters and telephone calls means a lot of work for the staff. However, we believe that this procedure is essential for creating a stable program that reaches the parents who need it most. We have found that a letter followed by a telephone call makes it far more likely that parents will come to the first meeting. At one point, we decided to make some small changes in our letter. Instead of promising the family that we would call within a few days, we asked them to call us. During the next two months, only 3% of the families that received a letter called in. This was in dramatic contrast to the response rate of over 50% that was generated by the letter plus telephone call procedure we used previously. After this experience, we returned to our original routine.

Organizing Meetings

A Typical First Meeting

Choose a time and date for the first meeting that fits in with the group leader's schedule. The first meeting is usually held at the group leader's house, and she provides coffee, tea, juice, and some sort of snack. Subsequent meetings are held at the homes of group members who take turns at being "host" and providing refreshments.

As the parents come in, they settle into chairs or sit on the floor. Having the babies there helps to break the ice—they immediately give everyone something to talk about. In any case, many parents simply wouldn't come without their babies (although we usually encourage people to find babysitters for older siblings, especially for the first meeting). Parents introduce themselves (stick-on name tags are helpful), and the group leader passes around copies of a list with each person's name, address, and telephone number and the babies' names and birthdates. The group leader's name and telephone number should also be on the list.

After the latecomers have settled in, the group leader starts the meeting by inviting parents in turn to tell a bit about themselves and their birth experiences. This might take an hour or so and, by the end, people usually feel that they have shared quite a lot with one another. After everyone has had a chance to talk, the group leader describes her own birth experience(s) and goes on to tell about Birth to Three, why it was set up, and what it has to offer. The community resources that are listed on the poster are reviewed and the leader encourages everyone to participate in planning topics for discussion at later meetings. Then she might ask whether there are any questions or issues that anyone would like to bring up regarding baby care (crying, feeding, sleeping, etc.), the parents' well-being, or the situation at home. If there is time, other questions can be used to generate discussion such as, "How does the reality of having a baby compare with your expectations?" or "Are you managing to structure your day so that you get some time to yourself?" Just about everyone has something to say about these topics. Usually one-and-a-half to two hours is about the right amount of time for the first meeting; later meetings are generally a little longer. Before the end of the first meeting have the group decide whether meetings should be held every week or every other week and choose a convenient time and day of the week. Everyone should also agree on a topic and location for the next meeting.

For awhile the group leader calls the parents in her groups between meetings to remind them about the next meeting (especially if the parent hasn't attended the last one) and to ask about how things are going. After the group has met several times, a telephone tree of some kind is usually organized. The group leader might call five parents and have each of them call one or two others. This is a good way to share the task of contacting everyone and encourages group members to get better acquainted and feel responsible for one another.

In special circumstances, the group leader may persist in calling someone for months even if that person has never, or rarely, attended meetings. One woman, whose baby was born with cataracts in both eyes, was unable to come to a meeting for six months because of her baby's frequent medical treatments. However, she definitely appreciated regular phone calls and the chance to talk about what she was going through.

Later Meetings

The discussion for the second meeting can be focused on the abundance of books and magazines on child development and parenting that many of us have in our personal libraries. Members are asked to bring in anything relevant that they have read recently. At the meeting, parents describe what they have brought, pass it around the group, and comment on what they liked or didn't like about the book or magazine. It is important to respect the opinions that are expressed even when they conflict with those of the "experts." This format usually prompts lively discussions in which parents express their personal philosophies regarding bringing up children.

We try to examine the materials critically, raise questions about the information and outlooks they provide on child-rearing, and talk about the ways in which families are depicted (especially in the magazines). Keeping these conversations going is seldom a problem. However, the group leader needs to make sure that all members have an opportunity to speak (inviting each person in the circle to talk in turn guarantees that no one is left out). It is also important that she help the group to maintain a respectful atmosphere so that members are comfortable expressing their views.

Subsequent meetings may deal with topics such as baby massage (see Leboyer's book, *Loving Hands*) or postpartum exercises, babies' cognitive and emotional development, how the couple's relationship has changed since the baby was born, and bloopers we've made in caring for the baby. It is often a good idea for the leader to volunteer a blooper first. For example, one of us nursed her first child through a hot summer and was told by her doctor to give the baby water between feedings. She tried this but was puzzled to find the same amount of water in the bottle after 20 minutes of energetic sucking. This went on until someone finally pointed out that she had to make a hole in the nipple! Stories like these relax everyone and almost every parent will admit making some sort of memorable blunder.

In the beginning, we zealously photocopied interesting articles for group discussion and distributed them to group members. As the number of groups multiplied, so did the cost involved in making copies of material. A more efficient system is to assemble loose-leaf notebooks (which can be updated periodically) containing articles organized around topics such as nutrition, family life, play activities with children, discipline, and so on. A notebook is prepared for each group to circulate among its members. When everyone is finished with it, it is passed on to a new group.

As the babies start becoming mobile, many groups find

that carrying on a discussion becomes a challenge. At least one parent always seems occupied with trying to separate two tussling babies, extricating a child from trouble, or chasing down a child who has wandered off. One solution to the problem is for the group to arrange for one or two babysitters to take charge while the parents meet in another part of the house. Another approach is to meet alternately in the morning with the babies and in the evening without babies (perhaps going to a restaurant together for coffee, dessert, and some adult conversation).

People typically come to meetings eager for a chance to talk. Some of the richest, most satisfying discussions we have in Birth to Three groups are generated by asking each person to report on what has been going on in her or his life lately. All sorts of topics are brought up: problems in a marriage, a suspected pregnancy, an impending visit by a mother or mother-in-law, or a miserable night with a restless baby. These discussions work best when each person is given a chance to talk, with the focus moving along to the next person after the group has had a chance to comment or share similar experiences. It is important that no one dominates or interrupts the discussion, that people's feelings are respected, and that all information shared with the group is kept confidential. Conversations between individuals that are not part of the group discussions should be kept to a minimum. The group leader should encourage people to respond to one another and not wait for the leader to assert her own viewpoint. It is important to teach group members to support and rely on each other so that they can ultimately function as a group without the help of the leader.

Most groups continue meeting (once a week to once a month) for one-and-a-half to two years. There are many groups, however, that stay together longer because new babies are born into the group. The resulting core of veteran members provides stability as some people leave and others join. Play groups and babysitting co-ops often grow out of Birth to Three groups and continue to function after the group stops meeting formally.

Volunteer Group Leaders

A group leader might meet with as many as four or five groups on different mornings of the week. As new groups are started she gradually phases herself out of "old" groups. At the first meeting, the group leader should explain that she will be able to come to meetings for about five months. After the group has been meeting for about four months, she asks for one, two, or even three people who would be willing to act as volunteer group leaders.

Women who become volunteer group leaders have various degrees of experience in leading groups. In some cases, they have never assumed a leadership role before or participated in other groups. These women often take pride in learning the skills that are necessary to be effective helpers, organizers, and facilitators. Other women who become volunteer leaders work professionally as social workers, teachers, and so on. It is usually very easy for them to make the transition from the role of group member to group leader. After volunteers have been selected and trained to lead the group, the responsibilities of the group leader are gradually shifted onto their shoulders. The original group leader continues to attend the first two or three volunteer-led meetings to ease the transition, and then calls the volunteer leader every two weeks or so to check on how things are going and to offer suggestions. After a few months, the responsibility of keeping track of volunteer group leaders is turned over to the volunteer coordinator. Additional training and supervision are also provided for volunteer group leaders during in-service meetings that are scheduled by the volunteer coordinator. These meetings are an opportunity for volunteer group leaders to acquire new skills and receive further instruction on how to handle groups.

By the time the original group leader begins to withdraw, the group is well established and the volunteer leader's job is relatively easy and straightforward. The ground rules are understood, the members know each other well, and conversation flows smoothly. The volunteer leader's main responsibilities are calling members between meetings and supervising the telephone tree, running meetings, and keeping the discussion focused. In some groups, each member takes a turn leading the meetings so that everyone has a chance at it. In this case it may be a good idea to ask someone to volunteer to take responsibility for inviting speakers to address the group. These variations (and others) are all workable arrangements that tend to make everyone feel more involved.

It is also possible for someone who has not previously been a member of a Birth to Three group to become a group leader. Sometimes a mother outside the Eugene-Springfield target areas (or living in another part of the county altogether) calls in to say that she and several other women in her area would like to join a Birth to Three group. Under these circumstances we might invite her to become a volunteer group leader and start her own group with some help from us. The volunteer coordinator at Birth to Three mails application forms to prospective volunteers and interviews them. Applicants must attend the meetings of at least three different groups to get a feeling for the program. If they are still interested, they are required to come to a training session for volunteers before they lead their first group.

Prospective group leaders are trained to lead Birth to Three groups during day-long training workshops held several times each year. At these workshops, prospective leaders learn about selected topics in child development and small group dynamics. Birth to Three's philosophy and organizational structure are explained in some detail so that the volunteer leaders understand the program's history and purpose. Other facilities and resources for new parents that are available in the community are also reviewed. Finally, the group leaders are taught how to identify the signs of child abuse and neglect, and what to do if evidence of these problems is noticed in their group.

Perhaps the most important goal of training workshops is to help the prospective group leaders improve their leadership and communication skills. Good communication skills are developed by participating in exercises that are designed to teach individuals how to listen to others empathetically and give nonjudgmental feedback. Group leader trainees are taught to present themselves as well-informed peers, rather than as experts evaluating the views of other group members. By being open to differing opinions, the leader can create a comfortable atmosphere in which group members feel accepted and understood. By role-playing problem situations in the training workshops, prospective leaders learn how to resolve problems constructively. Above all, group leaders are taught to respect each member's individuality. They are encouraged to use an assertive and yet democratic style of leadership that is in keeping with Birth to Three's philosophy and goals.

Volunteers who are new to the program and group members who are taking over the leader's responsibilities for their own group are expected to attend these training workshops. After the initial training session, volunteer group leaders meet together one evening every other month. These meetings provide an opportunity to hear about the activities of other groups and discuss solutions to problems. Speakers are also invited to these meetings to lecture on topics such as child abuse, marriage counseling, or group process. These inservice training sessions give the group leaders skills and information that they can take back to their groups.

In many ways, the growth of a Birth to Three program beyond one or two support groups depends upon the dedication and efforts of volunteer group leaders. As your Birth to Three program becomes better known in the community, more people expect to be able to join a group in their area, but staff members may quickly become overwhelmed with the extra work that new groups require. One possibility is for the staff to concentrate on leading groups in the target areas and groups for "at-risk" parents (for example, groups for teenage parents and potentially abusive parents). As the program continues to expand, more volunteers can be recruited to lead groups. Volunteers can be used to organize groups for fathers, parents with toddlers (for which there is an extraordinary demand), parents with newborn babies in nontarget areas, and parents living in rural communities. Volunteers can also co-lead, with staff members, groups for high-risk parents and teenage parents, or serve as volunteer "friends," matched one-to-one with teenage parents. With proper training and supervision, volunteer group leaders can make it possible for your program to provide services to the entire community.

CHAPTER 5

Providing Additional Services

In addition to organizing parent groups, Birth to Three in Eugene offers several other services to parents in the community. These include a community resources poster, peer counseling, a newsletter, educational events, and parenting classes. We sponsor an educational series for parents with toddlers, a rural program, groups for single parents, and "Birth to Three for Teenage Parents." A series for parents under stress called "Make Parenting a Pleasure" is also conducted in collaboration with the Eugene Family YMCA. This chapter describes these services in detail. The range of services that your own group provides will, of course, depend upon its size and resources. At first, it is probably best to concentrate on organizing and running the parent support groups that are the core of Birth to Three. Once several groups have been successfully set into motion, these other options may be something to consider.

The Community Resources Poster

One of the first projects we undertook was to assemble a list of community services available to new parents. After talking to parents it became obvious that there was a need for this sort of directory; at one time or another, most families need specialized help. Yet, even people who generally know about their community have difficulty finding services that are designed especially for parents. Telephone listings often do not state clearly the services that are offered by businesses and agencies, and some volunteer organizations are not listed at all (for example, in Eugene there is no telephone listing for La Leche League counselors or the local chapter of Mothers of Twins). In addition to names and telephone numbers, the directory that we compiled included a short description of the services offered by each organization. To make it easy to use, we designed the directory as a poster that was attractive enough to be displayed in parents' homes. We thought that a poster placed on a wall or refrigerator door would also be less likely to be lost or thrown away with the offers for diaper service and color portraits that arrive along with a new baby.

The poster provided the telephone numbers for specialized volunteer services such as La Leche League counselors who advise on breastfeeding, support groups for women who have had Cesarean births, and the local contact person for Parents Anonymous. It listed organizations that help parents with infants who have developmental handicaps, public health department services, child-care referral agencies, sources of inexpensive medical and mental health care for families, and the telephone number of the poison-control center. In each case, we asked the agency or organization to write a short description of their services; where this failed we drafted a description and asked them to approve it. Finally, we added a list of library programs and educational events for children, some recommended readings for new parents, and information about Birth to Three.

After we had compiled this information, we had to transform it into a finished product. This was made possible by two significant contributions. The public health department donated the services of its graphic artist to design the poster, and a local printer produced 3,000 copies at no charge (his contribution was acknowledged at the bottom of the poster). This gave us enough copies of the poster to cover the expected births in the Eugene-Springfield area for about one year.

We had decided that the best method of distribution would be through maternity hospitals, birthing centers, and lay-midwives in Eugene and Springfield. Generally when each new mother leaves the hospital with her baby she is given a bag full of formula samples, lotion and baby oil, coupons to be redeemed at local stores, and miscellaneous baby-care pamphlets. We wanted the nurses to put a rolled-up Birth to Three poster in those bags. The pediatrician and nurse-midwife on our Board talked with the pediatric and obstetric committees at the hospitals, and so did we. After an initial trial period, distribution of the posters has become part of the hospital routine. When approaching the hospitals in the way we did, you may find it helpful to cite the precedent that we set to convince hospital personnel that this is an acceptable practice. We visited the family practitioners, obstetricians, and pediatricians in Eugene and Springfield to tell them what we were doing and give them posters for their offices. Posters were put on display at the library, at social service and mental health agency offices, and on community center bulletin boards. The poster has proven to be very effective in generating responses from parents. We started to receive phone calls from parents on a regular basis almost immediately. From the very beginning, the response to the poster was an indication that our services were really needed.

The poster continues to be one of our most cost-effective means for contacting new parents. We revise it annually to make sure that the information is up-to-date. A volunteer is assigned the task of routinely checking the supply of posters at the hospitals and other agencies and keeping the obstetric nurses and other hospital professionals in touch with new developments in Birth to Three.

Peer Counseling

New parents often feel that they need to talk to someone who understands their situation. Sometimes they need information, and at other times just a sympathetic ear. In most cases, talking to another parent can make an important difference. But a crisis or a pressing question cannot always wait for a regularly scheduled meeting. For this reason, we decided to set up a "warm line" peer-counseling service. Because our organization was still small and had no office, the telephone was installed in someone's home. Later, we used call forwarding to rotate the responsibility for peer counseling to different staff members.

Our very first call was from a distressed mother with an 11-month-old baby. "He's holding onto my legs all the time. He cries every time I move away from him. I feel like picking him up and throwing him against the wall." After about 40 minutes she calmed down and both she and the staff member felt all right about hanging up. The staff person called back a few days later and the mother said that she was feeling much better.

Encouragement, humor, candor, good listening, and practical suggestions are all helpful in talking to upset parents. Sometimes, reassurance and sympathy are all that is needed. In other cases the caller needs someone to help her define and resolve problems. The parents who call should be encouraged to call again whenever they need to. The peer counselor should always call a troubled parent back two or three days later to make sure that things are improving.

Some calls lead to long and repeated interactions. Others, such as someone calling from a phone booth to ask where to go for pregnancy counseling, are a brief, one-time contact. We talk to some mothers on the telephone periodically for several months before finally meeting them in person—if we ever do. A father whose wife died shortly after the birth of their baby used to call every so often and, even though he only came to one Birth to Three meeting, it was important for him to have someone to talk to.

In some cases, the counselor should refer the caller elsewhere for treatment or advice. One new mother had a temperature that would not go away and she felt awful. In addition, her two-week-old baby seemed to need to nurse all day long. "My baby screams whenever he isn't eating. Why did he turn out this way? I was so careful during the pregnancy—I did all the right things. I know that I shouldn't be letting him cry, but the only way to keep him quiet is to let him nurse, and my breasts really hurt from all the sucking." She was so tired and uncomfortable that it was difficult for her to organize her thoughts. On the day that she finally called in for help, she could hardly take care of her own physical and emotional needs, let alone tend to a demanding infant. The peer counselor suggested that the best thing she could do for her baby was to look after her own health immediately and encouraged her to make an appointment with her obstetrician. Family Services was contacted to arrange for a homemaker-aide to make some meals to put in the refrigerator, clean up a bit, and help take care of the baby while the mother slept.

Occasionally, a doctor or a counselor will ask us to call a patient or client. A young mother of a one-year-old, married to a foreign student at the university, knew almost no one in town. She spoke very little English and the family lived in an apartment building where there were no other children. When she visited her pediatrician he told her about Birth to Three and asked if she would mind if someone from the organization gave her a call. When we phoned, she said she was homesick and depressed; she was spending all day in bed, didn't feel like getting up, and didn't know what to do with the baby. The baby cried a lot and she couldn't seem to amuse him. Although she felt it would be helpful to see other mothers with children the same age, she didn't know any and couldn't drive to places where she might meet them. The peer counselor called the volunteer who was leading the nearest group for one-year-olds and arranged for the mother to be invited to their next meeting. As it turned out, a member of the group lived close by and offered to give her a ride. They eventually became good friends and started to exchange some babysitting time. The mother attended Birth to Three meetings regularly, her English improved, and as she met some new people she began to feel better about her own situation.

It often seemed as though people were just waiting for a decent hour to call, and the phone would begin to ring at precisely 8:30 or 9:00 a.m. By the time we got an office, we were glad to be able to install the phone where a staff person or volunteer answered it during normal office hours. We also purchased an answering machine to record the calls that came in after office hours. Although we liked the idea of always being available, it was more than we could handle. Our current "compromise" is to receive calls at home only from members of groups that we are personally leading.

The Newsletter

A newsletter is an excellent way to keep parents in touch with the activities of the entire Birth to Three organization. The newsletter tells them about forthcoming events, provides access to community resources, educates readers, shares the experiences of other members, and builds a feeling of belonging to something larger than one's own group. Because it provides a concrete record of the organization, the newsletter can also be an important public relations tool. It helps Birth to Three make an impression on people who do not use the peer-counseling services or belong to groups.

There are many successful approaches to publishing a newsletter. It can be a monthly, bimonthly, or quarterly publication. It could be photocopied on a single 8½"x11" sheet, or printed on several 11"x17" sheets that are folded into a booklet or brochure. Many different topics can be addressed. To give you some idea of what a relatively comprehensive newsletter might be like, we will describe our own.

Birth to Three's newsletter is a bimonthly publication that is mailed to approximately 1100 households every other month. Our mailing list is made up of local physicians, social service agencies, libraries, funding sources, and representatives of local government in addition to members of our groups. The newsletter is printed on two 11"x17" sheets that are folded twice so that the newsletter can be stapled closed brochure-style for mailing (in printer's terms this is called a "self-mailer"). It is printed on orange paper and the Birth to Three logo appears prominently on the front so that the newsletter can be easily distinguished from the daily mail. In many households, the newsletter's arrival is announced by the resident two-year-old helper.

The following sections appear in each newsletter:

1) Feature articles on topics such as car-seat safety, ways to structure time efficiently, discipline, nutrition, and language development. Some of these articles are reprinted from other sources, but most of them are original articles written by our newsletter editor.

2) Book reviews.

3) A bulletin board for upcoming Birth to Three activities.

4) A calendar of educational events, classes, and programs sponsored by other community organizations for parents of young children.

5) Classified ads. Because parents use a lot of goods and services, it is relatively easy to sell advertising space in the newsletter. Retailers routinely place advertisements in the newsletter, as do child-care providers who want to list their

services, and parents who want to buy or sell baby equipment.

The newsletter should be written for an audience of parents with diverse educational backgrounds and attitudes toward parenting. Achieving the right style is not always easy—the tone should be serious but not formal, informative but non-technical, and so on. Try not to be intimidated; the important thing is to recruit some talent and get started! Do the best that you can and refine your newsletter as you go along.

Write to us at the address given on page 42 for information on subscribing to the newsletter and purchasing back issues. If you decide to follow this sort of format, don't take on too much too soon. Start with one or two sections that are relatively easy to put together. Your first issue may have "just" a list of upcoming Birth to Three meetings, community activities, and a few classified ads. The newsletter can then be expanded along with the organization. It is worthwhile to pay some attention to how the newsletter looks. An attractive format will make it easier to find subscribers, advertisers, and even sponsors for the organization. Once there are quite a few people involved in your program, it is usually possible to find someone who is willing to volunteer graphic services or publishing skills to help you get started. Subscriptions to the newsletter and classified advertising from local businesses (diaper services, etc.) will help to defray printing and mailing costs. Contacting businesses about advertising space also helps to make your organization known in the community.

Birth to Three board members, volunteer group leaders, physicians, and social service agencies receive the newsletter free. New parents in targeted areas are added to the newsletter mailing list automatically. They receive one issue free and then are asked to subscribe if they want to continue receiving it. Most of our newsletters are mailed to individuals and groups who subscribe on an annual basis. These include

70

members of Birth to Three groups, as well as individuals and organizations around the country who have heard about the program.

Parenting Classes

After Birth to Three organized support groups for about a year, we decided to offer parenting classes as a way to get more parents involved in our program. In this more structured format, 10 to 15 parents enroll in a series of eight classes which meet once each week for two hours. Some participants would rather attend parenting classes than support group meetings because they want specific information or because they are unaccustomed to talking about themselves in a group. When possible, meetings are held in the same place each week. One of the best facilities for our meetings was a church that offered us a large, comfortable meeting room and an adjoining playroom where a babysitter could take care of toddlers who had come along.

At the beginning of every meeting, time is set aside for participants to share the events of the past week. During the class session, they are encouraged to talk about their ideas and experiences. This helps to bring the group members closer together and creates an easy, informal atmosphere. Each meeting is dedicated to a particular topic such as "The Challenge Facing New Parents," "Feeding, Sleeping, and Crying," "Stages of Development through the First Year," "Socialization and Discipline," and so on. Discussion outlines and supplementary reading materials for eight classes are provided in Chapter 7 of this book.

Parenting classes are usually led by a Birth to Three staff member and a volunteer co-leader. A comfortable, relaxed atmosphere makes it easy for parents to ask questions and talk candidly. In most cases, a support group is formed at the end of the eighth class—by then the parents know and trust each other well enough to want to continue meeting. The co-leaders help form the support group and continue to meet with its members for several months, helping them divide up tasks, choose discussion topics, organize meetings, and eventually select a volunteer leader.

Educational Events

Each month, we sponsor an educational event for the community. The format of these events varies, ranging from a lecture by an expert in child development, to a panel discussion on discipline, to a "parent fair" jointly sponsored with other agencies. Topics have included "Winter Illnesses and Small Children," "Differences in Infant Temperament," and "The First Six Months: From the Baby's and the Parents' Perspective." A more complete list is provided in Appendix 7.1. These educational events are publicized through our newsletter, public-service radio announcements, and listings in the local newspaper's "Community Events" column. Free meeting space is often provided by banks, libraries, and schools.

Educational events serve several functions. They supplement discussions in the support groups by drawing on greater expertise than the leader and members have to offer. They provide the speaker with an opportunity to address a large and motivated audience, and they help train volunteer leaders by providing them with information to be relayed to their groups. They also advertise the program as a whole and provide a way to recruit new members. Some people who are reluctant to go to a group meeting may come to a public lecture to get a feeling for what Birth to Three is all about.

Variations on the Theme

In this section we describe some adaptations of the Birth to Three model that we have developed to provide for the needs of parents in special circumstances. These include support groups for single parents, "Birth to Three for Teenage

72

Parents," and a series called "Make Parenting a Pleasure" for parents under stress. We have also put together a program for parents with toddlers, and we organize support groups for parents in rural areas. While the format used in these groups and meetings is similar to the "standard" format that we have described in Chapter 4, there are important differences in the procedures for recruiting parents, organizing meetings, and in the material covered. If you are interested in the curriculum materials that we have developed for these adaptations of our program, write to us for more information (our address for correspondence appears on page 42).

Single Parents

The special problems of single parents (most of whom are women) include having sole responsibility for the child, lack of money, and little free time. Not having a partner generally means there is no other adult to help make decisions and offer emotional support. The entire burden falls on the mother, and it can be overwhelming. She may find herself distanced from her friends and in conflict with her own parents, especially if she is again dependent on them. Living alone, meeting and dating men, and defining relationships are some of the concerns of single mothers. Typically, there are issues still unresolved between the mother and the father of the child such as divorce, custody, child support, and abuse. The mother may feel torn between trying to push the father out of her life and hoping to get him more involved with the child and herself.

Money is almost always an issue for women who are single parents. Depending on welfare does not provide financial security, and if the woman chooses to work full time she may find that her economic situation is hardly improved, while she scarcely sees her child.

Some single mothers invest all of their emotional energy in their children. If this is carried to an extreme, it becomes diffi-

73

cult for the mother to discipline her child. She may alternate between feeling resentment toward the child for taking control of her life, and feeling guilty for not being able to do more. Regular contact with other parents in similar circumstances always broadens a person's perspective and may help a single parent to make constructive changes in her life. A single parents' group enables mothers to share resources, exchange child care, and receive emotional support from others who understand their situation.

Because of the stress and complicated circumstances in the lives of most single parents with small children, it is difficult to get them to make a commitment to join a parents' group like Birth to Three. For this reason, the staff of Birth to Three makes a special effort to reach single parents. We spend a lot of time counseling on the telephone and referring single parents to other agencies for services that we cannot provide. We also make home visits and arrange transportation for parents who have no means of getting to meetings. Generally, things seem to go more smoothly when a group for single parents meets in a public meeting room that has been made available by a church or school rather than in someone's home. The place should be easily accessible by public transportation, and if babysitting can be offered in an adjoining room, this is a big help. We have found that it is best to have two staff members or volunteers co-lead a single parents' group, and at least one of those leaders should be a single parent herself.

Teenage Parents

The period following the birth of a baby can be difficult for any family, but for teenage parents, the stress of new parenthood can be magnified by low self-esteem, poor coping skills, isolation, and poverty. This places both the parent and the child at risk for developing long-term, serious problems. Teenage parents are still trying to handle the problem of adolescence and may need considerable assistance and emotional support in dealing with their daily responsibilities in order to become productive adults. Local programs for teenage parents already include specialized high school courses, counseling and homemaker services, and nutrition and family-planning clinics. However, most adolescent parents make little use of these programs because they don't know about them, they feel awkward about being "treated" by social service agencies, or because other circumstances make it difficult to attend meetings.

Birth to Three provides a comprehensive support network for teenage parents by working closely with other community organizations. In order to encourage teenage parents to attend meetings and help them get to other appointments, and to provide a role model, moral support, and occasional "relief" outings, each teenager who is interested is matched with a volunteer "friend." These are somewhat older mothers who are participating in their own Birth to Three groups or who may have been teenage parents themselves. Proper screening, followed by ongoing training in communication skills and an understanding of adolescent development, are essential for these volunteers. Second-hand clothing and baby equipment are often donated to the teenage parents by members of other Birth to Three groups. Recreational outings with the babies, such as picnics or trips to the zoo, help to meet the teenage parents' needs for fun and companionship.

The support groups provide information about career and educational opportunities, access to existing services in the community, a chance to see other mothers, the opportunity to develop coping and communication skills, assistance with personal health and household management, and education about parenting to reduce the risk of child abuse and neglect. Themes for discussion include setting and achieving goals, family planning, managing money, housing problems, school, anger, feelings of alienation, personal histories of family violence, and drug and alcohol problems. For adolescent parents, many of whom are still absorbed in sorting out complicated relationships with their own parents, participating in a special Birth to Three program can help give them the feeling that their parenthood is valued and respected.

Parents Under Stress

A Birth to Three program called "Make Parenting a Pleasure" is offered in collaboration with the Eugene Family YMCA to parents who are under stress and potentially abusive. As a prevention program, "Make Parenting a Pleasure" addresses the needs of parents who feel that they are going through a particularly rough spell with their children. Most of the participants are single parents, unemployed, low-income, or were themselves abused as children. The program offers support groups and parent-education classes, free child care during class sessions, and opportunities to use YMCA exercise facilities and take part in the classes offered there. Each class consists of eight weekly two-hour sessions, co-led by a staff person and a trained volunteer. At the conclusion of the eight-week series, the volunteer continues to meet with the parents in a support group.

"Make Parenting a Pleasure" appeals to parents who might not otherwise attend a parenting class. It is nonstigmatizing (we deliberately chose an upbeat name for the series that wouldn't alienate the people we were hoping to serve), has a positive image (the YMCA is a pleasant meeting place), develops a peer-support network, and educates parents. The program has received the support of social service agencies in the community that work with parents under stress. Parents are referred to the program by local family counseling agencies, physicians, the Children's Protective Services Division, and the local battered women's shelter. The community-wide coordination between referring agencies and the "Make Parenting a Pleasure" series, and the collaboration between Birth to Three and the YMCA, encouraged several foundations to

76

contribute seed money to start the program. We think that this sort of collaboration can be arranged in any community where active parents' groups and community centers such as the YMCA are interested in thinking creatively about the problem of child abuse and pooling their resources to help solve it.

Social service agency budget cuts have especially affected parents under stress during the past few years. By carefully utilizing volunteers, this sort of program is able to extend child abuse prevention service delivery through peer-counseling and peer-support groups to large numbers of high-risk parents. For potentially abusive parents, support groups form a bridge to agencies that can provide more intensive care. Often, when the situation of these parents has stabilized somewhat, they are able to use the groups as a source of continuing support. Some of the most important activities occur between meetings. Group members offer one another material and emotional assistance in times of crisis, doing for one another what the extended family did for its members. This saves the community the costs (both financial and social) of supporting families who would otherwise be hard-pressed to cope on their own.

The Toddler Program

Some parents who enjoyed their children as infants feel inadequate when it comes time to care for a walking, talking, physically and emotionally volatile toddler. The period when infants become mobile is viewed by some child developmentalists as a watershed period. At this stage children no longer have to wait for the world to come to them—they can move on their own and act upon it at will. According to Piaget, this is the beginning of the sensorimotor period when children learn through their senses and through movement. In general, it is a fascinating but difficult stage for both the child and the parent. The child often fluctuates between feeling powerful and powerless and, ironically, so does the parent. It helps if parents try to understand the world of the toddler and the normal developmental characteristics of this period. Then parents are in a better position to use their creativity and problem-solving abilities to work with the child instead of being in conflict with him or her. The aim of the toddler program is to help parents expand their repertoire of parenting skills during a developmental phase that is particularly frustrating in many families.

The toddler program is set up as a series of 10 two-hour sessions that are held once a week. The class is generally broken into two one-hour periods. During the first period, the children and the parents are together and the parents learn "nursery-school teacher" skills in an informal setting. Play activities and games are made available including blocks and floor toys (such as cars, push toys, and trucks), a playhouse (with dolls, sinks, stoves, tables, and dishes), table games (such as simple puzzles, sorting boxes, peg boards, and play-dough), easel and paints, and rocking horses. This is usually the first play-group experience for most of the children, and it gives the parents a chance to see their own child in a different setting, as well as a chance to observe other children and other parenting styles. A Birth to Three staff person models appropriate ways to work with the children, talks with the parents informally, and helps the parents to set up and put away the play materials. The last 20 minutes of parent-child time is spent singing songs and playing circle games, and the children have a snack. The parents sit in a circle on the floor with the children on their laps. A few children wander around, but as the songs and the ritual become more familiar, these children usually want to participate, too. This is an opportunity for the parents to learn songs and games to use with their children later, when a song might defuse a tense moment, help make the time go faster in the car, or take the conflict out of getting ready for bed. For the parent and toddler it is an enjoyable time spent together, during a phase when some parents are hard-pressed to find many such moments.

After the first hour, the parents move to another room for a discussion and the children continue to play, supervised by two paid child-care workers and one or two parents. The responsibility is rotated among the parents, and each is required to supervise the children once during the 10-week period.

Some time is allowed at the beginning of each meeting for informal exchanges of news and help with current problems. The discussion is then focused on the topic that has been chosen for that week (a list of topics appears in Appendix 5.1). The Birth to Three staff person acts as facilitator by opening the discussion with pertinent information or a group exercise. The group members share their experiences and ideas on the topic. It is hoped that by clarifying the issues, brainstorming ideas, and understanding the stages of child development, parents will come up with solutions to some of the problems that they have been experiencing, feel more competent, and derive more pleasure from interacting with their toddler.

Rural Groups

In rural communities, mothers of small children are usually more isolated than they would be in larger towns and cities. Mothers calling Birth to Three from rural areas are often so eager to see other mothers and babies that in many cases the thought of driving 15 or 20 miles to town is not too discouraging. With trained volunteers we have been able to start groups in a dozen rural communities, some as far as 50 miles away. These volunteers are mothers who would rather cultivate a local support network than commute to a distant one.

Volunteer leaders in rural communities are required to attend the same training workshop that is required of local volunteers, and they are strongly urged to attend the bimonthly in-service training meetings for volunteers, as well. Volunteer leaders in rural communities recruit members with notices in public places and doctors' offices, public service announcements on local radio stations, and articles in local newspapers. After a while, word of mouth does the rest. Birth to Three's volunteer coordinator helps each set of leaders generate a resource poster for their community and search out local speakers who can be invited to meetings. The volunteer coordinator attends the first one or two of the groups' meetings and calls the leaders regularly to help with any problems that arise.

Rural groups usually do not consist of parents with babies of the same age, since in small communities there are generally not enough new babies born each month to form a group. Instead, the babies in these groups often range between infancy and three years of age or older, with many mothers bringing two children along. Under these conditions, the logistics of conducting a discussion can be tricky, and groups need to plan creative ways of occupying the kids so that meetings are satisfying rather than frustrating. In any group where there are small but mobile children of different ages, it is recommended that each of the mothers brings along toys, books, and snacks, or that one or two adults be appointed to take care of the older kids. It can be difficult to run groups like this, but the benefit of regular social contact for toddlers and parents is worth the effort.

CHAPTER 6

Setting Up an Organization

There are certain components common to all organizations regardless of the structure they are based on. This chapter describes some of these essential working parts and provides guidelines for adapting them to suit the needs of your organization. This material is important because most of the people who set up Birth to Three support groups will end up running an organization at some point in the development of their program. Some of these components, such as record keeping and fundraising, are also relevant for smaller groups. Additional topics to be covered in this chapter include writing a policies and procedures manual, leading staff meetings, preventing staff burn-out, setting up a board of directors, getting along with other organizations, networking, and evaluating the success of your program.

Record Keeping

A good record-keeping system is essential to every organization. It allows you to condense and save all of the detailed information that is generated by the day-to-day functioning of your program. A complete set of records also makes it easier for one staff member to take over or fill in for someone else. The following record-keeping suggestions can be scaled up or down depending on the size of your program, the obligations imposed on you by funding organizations or regulating agencies, and your own goals. The principles are generally the same regardless of the system you use.

Records need to be kept at several different levels. Copies of all outgoing correspondence and internal memos should be kept on file. The important details of each incoming phone call should be recorded in a notebook, describing who called, when, and why. Is the phone call from another agency referring a parent? Is it someone requesting information about your program? Is it a parent wanting to join a support group? Is it a mother having problems with her children? Your notes should be complete enough to reconstruct the topics covered in the conversation. This record helps you keep track of things and allows you to summarize your activities for funding agencies. They may want to know, for example, the number of people you have served and which agencies have used your services.

Each staff member or volunteer who organizes and leads a group should keep relatively detailed records about each of the members. An efficient way to do this is to write notes about each family on a 3x5 card. These cards can then be arranged alphabetically in an index card box for easy reference. Each group should have its own section in the box. For each family, record the name(s) of the parent(s), their address and telephone number, the name(s) and birthdate(s) of the child(ren), and how the parent(s) heard about the program (for example, referred by a physician, received a letter from Birth to Three inviting them to join, and so on). Every time a group leader calls a parent, a note should be made regarding

82

the date and the topic discussed. Any special circumstances that need to be followed up should be noted for future reference.

These files should, of course, be kept confidential. It is important to exercise professional discretion at all times—never repeat anything of a sensitive nature that you hear at a meeting or are told on the telephone in confidence. When describing your program never suggest that someone endorses it without their express permission to do so. Your records should be objective and fair so that a parent looking at his or her own card in your file would not be offended by whatever you have written.

In addition to keeping records of daily activities, it is a good idea to produce monthly, quarterly, or annual reports, even if this is not required by funding agencies. You should know how many people joined groups during the quarter, how many dropped out, and how many are currently attending meetings. What percentage of the parents you contacted actually joined a group (50% is considered excellent)? How many people use the various services of your program per year? How does this year compare with previous years? How many phone calls of each type does your organization receive per month (for example, crisis calls, referrals)? How successful has your organization been in accomplishing the goals it originally set for itself? A good set of records that are periodically reviewed and summarized will give you a means to answer these important questions.

A Policies and Procedures Manual

A manual describing the policies and procedures of your organization should be put together sometime during the first year of operation. There are several reasons for doing this. First, the process of writing the manual forces you to decide exactly how your organization will function, what structure it will adopt (horizontal *vs.* vertical), what your goals are, and how you expect to achieve them. Second, a well-written manual is a convenient way to introduce new staff members and volunteers to the workings of the organization. When problems arise, it provides rules and guidelines for resolving them, saving time and reducing frustration.

It is a good idea to assemble the policies and procedures manual in a loose-leaf binder so that sections can be added or deleted as the program grows and changes. City administrators and public and private nonprofit organizations should be able to offer you some suggestions for setting up a comprehensive policies and procedures manual. Your goal in writing the manual is to make it thorough enough that someone in another community could reconstruct your entire program by reading it.

A policies and procedures manual should include:
1) the history and philosophy of the organization
2) record-keeping guidelines
3) accounting and budgeting practices
4) personnel policies
5) volunteer training procedures
6) samples of the materials that are used (for example, a copy of your community resources poster, a sample newsletter, form letters for contacting parents, parent-education class outlines, and so on).

Fundraising

If the program is run by volunteers or offered by an established agency, fundraising may not be a pressing issue. Asking for donations and organizing an occasional rummage or bake sale may be all that is needed. The federal funding we received in the beginning allowed us to focus our efforts on program planning and providing services to new parents in the community. However, as the federal support was gradually decreased, we realized that we would have to become increasingly serious about fundraising. Our program has relied on a number of fundraising methods to keep going.

The most obvious place to start generating income is to charge a membership fee to parents who join support groups. At first, the staff at Birth to Three objected to the idea of charging a fee to belong to a program that is based on peer support. After much debate, however, we decided to charge an annual fee of $10 (the fee is now $30) for membership dues and a year's subscription to the Birth to Three newsletter. We give parents the option of paying the fee in installments, and parents with lower incomes pay a reduced fee if necessary. Instead of using a sliding-fee scale, the decision concerning how much to collect for dues is left up to the individual staff member and prospective group member. This system seems to be acceptable to the community and has worked reasonably well for us. No one is discouraged from joining a group because of cost, and those who can pay know that their money goes to support an organization that they care about.

Unfortunately, a quick calculation shows that charging $10 (or even $30) per member does not generate enough money to sustain an organization that is setting up and running neighborhood groups in all parts of the community, training volunteer leaders, producing a newsletter, staffing a peer-counseling telephone line, and sponsoring educational activities and parenting classes for the community at large. We needed to find other ways to raise money. The following is a list of fundraising schemes that we have found to be effective:

1) Once each year we ask the readers of our newsletter to contribute to our program. This direct appeal has proven surprisingly effective. Often, people who support the program are just waiting to be told that you need help before they make a contribution.

2) Our board of directors launches a two-month-long fundraising campaign once each year. Each board member promises to raise a specific amount (for example, $200 to $300) by whatever means he or she chooses. Some ask for

contributions from friends or colleagues, others throw parties at which guests pay $10 for dessert; still others "sell" weekends at their family's beach cabin to their friends. Usually we provide a list of suggestions to help them get started. Because almost no one genuinely enjoys fundraising, we try to make this as much fun as we can. Sometimes the board members are divided into teams to compete for prizes that are given to those who raise the most money.

3) For several years we held an annual Birth to Three rummage and bake sale. This event was publicized through the newsletter and other local media. Fliers were also posted in various locations by volunteers. Birth to Three members were asked to donate used toys, children's and adults' clothing, and other saleable items. Others baked cakes and cookies. Any items that were not sold were given to the local shelter for battered women.

4) We sell T-shirts and sweatshirts featuring the Birth to Three name and logo; they are available in infants', children's, and adults' sizes.

5) We have held jogathons and walkathons where each participant finds sponsors who are willing to pay a modest amount for each lap or mile that the participant completes. This worked well in our athletically inclined community until the market became saturated. It may still work for you.

6) We convinced a pizza restaurant with an indoor play area to stage a party for Birth to Three. Families paid for their meals and the proceeds were divided between Birth to Three and the restaurant. It was good public relations for the restaurant, a good money-raising scheme for Birth to Three, and a fun night out for the families who came.

7) Once we tried a fashion show, put together by a board member who is a successful women's clothing designer with her own shop. A popular children's clothing store co-sponsored the event, and Birth to Three members and their kids modeled the clothes. This extravaganza was held at a restaur-

ant; tickets were sold and dessert was served.

8) We have put together our own coupon book. We asked local business people (many of them Birth to Three members) to donate goods and services such as an hour or two of carpentry, a woman's haircut, an hour of legal advice, a lesson in breadmaking, a jogging suit for a two-year-old, and other necessities and frivolities. For the contributors this was a good way to introduce others to their services. The coupon book was sold for $20 and the money went directly to Birth to Three.

9) We hold an annual raffle for which local businesses and individuals are asked to donate prizes. Birth to Three members purchase tickets at $1 each, and also sell them to their friends. Prizes are offered as incentives to those who sell the most tickets.

10) We rely on donations of goods and services from local businesses to cut the costs of running our organization. For years, one printing company has supplied us with quality stationery and envelopes printed with our logo at no cost; this company also gives us a discount on the cost of printing our newsletter in exchange for advertising space in it. Another company has given us a discount on all of our photocopying. Yet another printed our first year's supply of Birth to Three posters free, with an acknowledgement to the company appearing at the bottom of the poster. Funds for reprinting the poster each year have been provided by a local civic group.

11) We routinely submit requests for funds to local foundations, government agencies, and large companies. In order to succeed you must be able to document a need or problem in your community that is addressed by your program. Your goals and program evaluation procedures must be clearly stated. Begin by investigating funding prospects and their priorities. Private foundations, government agencies, and corporations are perhaps your likeliest sources of large grants. Although this type of fundraising requires a lot of effort and

research, it should not be ignored. In many ways, the survival of our community-wide program has depended on our success in obtaining grants.

None of the many approaches to fundraising is particularly easy. In choosing a strategy (or set of strategies), it is important to use your people as effectively as possible. They have a limited amount of effort to give and you need to help each person find the best way to give it. The success of your program depends entirely upon the good will of your members and other supporters in the community. It is just as possible for these people to "burn out" as it is for your staff members. Make sure that they feel comfortable about what they are doing and that their efforts are paying off. Fundraising is a hard job, but our experience suggests that if you design a good program, you will have an excellent chance of finding adequate support for it.

Staff Meetings

After some experimenting, the staff at Birth to Three decided to meet every other Monday morning for two hours. Before each meeting, the convenor prepares the agenda and establishes approximate time limits for each item. The agenda is attached to a clipboard which is passed around at the beginning of every meeting so that everyone has a chance to write in additional agenda items. It is also the convenor's job to take notes, record the minutes of the meetings, and keep the meeting going and the discussion focused (sometimes this is easier said than done). The responsibility of being the convenor is rotated once each month among staff members.

In a service-oriented organization, staff members often spend very little time together. Most of our time is spent working in our own homes or the homes of other parents. Even when we are in the office, we are frequently on the telephone or taking care of routine business matters. To help keep the group together and prevent Birth to Three from be-

88

coming just a job we decided to "sacrifice" some time at staff meetings to check in with each other on a personal basis. Staff meetings typically start with an informal half hour in which everyone can talk about how she is doing. This helps us to continue to appreciate each other as people and not just as co-workers.

Staff meetings may be long or short, frequent or infrequent, depending on the size and structure of your organization. If your staff is large, then regular meetings may involve subcommittees so that the whole group does not have to get together too often. If policy and program planning are worked out by the entire staff, then meetings will take longer than they do in organizations where one or two people are responsible for making decisions. Many of the details of your staff meetings will work themselves out as your organization unfolds.

Staff Burn-Out

Giving support to new parents takes a lot of time and energy. When this is combined with the effort that is required to keep your organization going, you and your staff can quickly become emotionally and physically drained. It always seems like there is too much to do, especially in the beginning, and there never seems to be a good time to take a day or two off to compensate for the overtime hours that you put in. If precautions are not taken, these factors can quickly lead to staff burn-out. It is important to prioritize the organization's goals and impose limits on your individual and collective efforts—when staff members regularly work excessive overtime, the organization's future is probably in jeopardy.

Another way to prevent burn-out is to maintain good relations among staff members. If people work well together, then everyone's job becomes easier and more enjoyable. Co-workers who know and care about each other can tell when rest, moral support, or technical help are needed by others. This sort of closeness and rapport does not, however, develop spontaneously among staff members and steps should be taken to create and maintain it. We have found that spending time together as a group outside the work situation cultivates good staff relations.

When things seem overwhelming, it is easy to forget why you are doing the work. Remind one another about the importance of your program to new parents in the community. You are, after all, helping parents to raise children who are healthy and well cared for. Convert this long-term satisfaction into more immediate rewards by letting staff members know that their work is appreciated. When someone does a good job, make sure he or she receives some positive feedback. Some reassurance, support, and words of encouragement and praise at the right times can make a lot of difference in how your staff feels about their work.

Setting Up a Board of Directors

If your organization decides to incorporate (as either a profit-making or nonprofit structure), you will be required to set up an advisory board or board of directors. The purpose of a board of directors is to provide guidance in policy-making and program development, offer technical assistance with budgeting, and help with fundraising activities. The individuals you select for your board of directors should be able to represent your program in a favorable light in the community and lend credibility to it by their professional stature, influence, and personal qualifications. A board of directors for an organization that addresses the needs of new parents should include pediatricians, obstetricians, gynecologists, or family practitioners; nurses, nurse practitioners, or certified nurse-midwives; lawyers; psychologists or counselors; accountants; people active in local politics; educators and university faculty members; business people (especially those serving women and children); and parents and volunteers in the program.

Prospective board members should be people who give good advice and are easy to work with. It is important for them to respect your goals and believe that you have the ability to achieve them.

Getting Along with Other Organizations

It is always a good idea to develop the best possible relations with other community programs that provide services to families. Avoid antagonizing other organizations by publicly criticizing their work or philosophy. This reflects poorly on you and erodes the good will that makes it possible for organizations working in the same area to help each other achieve common goals. Contact other groups and find out how you can work together. One obvious way is to refer parents to (and take referrals from) other agencies and organizations in the community that work with parents. Keep these people informed about new developments in your program. Make arrangements to speak to the staff of other organizations so that they know about the services you offer; talk to community groups and clubs, to mental health and health care professionals. The time that it takes is a worthwhile investment in your organization's future.

Networking

The term "networking" means working with other organizations to achieve common goals. An easy way to do this is to plan cooperative educational and fundraising events with other local organizations. A street fair or a children's carnival is more likely to be successful if several nonprofit organizations work on it together. In a similar vein, you might want to consider forming an association of nonprofit organizations to lobby for changes in the way that city funds are allocated to community-based programs. This sort of cooperation can definitely enhance the impact of your organization on the community.

If there are other parent-oriented organizations or groups in your area (including Birth to Three groups), stay in touch with one another. Make it a point to know about the activities they are sponsoring so that you can take part in them. When you put together a special event such as a lecture series for parents, let other groups know about it in advance so that they can participate in it. Share lecturers who are willing to give occasional talks to parent groups. Think creatively about ways to work with people and organizations at many different levels in your community.

Evaluation

An important part of running an effective program is continually evaluating how well it is achieving its goals. The feedback generated by periodic evaluations will help you to identify which components are working well and which need attention. The information generated can also be used to convince funding sources that your program is cost-effective and worthwhile. In some cases program evaluation may even be required as a condition for receiving support from private foundations and government agencies. Our experience suggests that some sort of evaluation procedure should be developed early in the life of your organization. This will insure that you have a record of how your organization has changed over time and will give you a place to start in designing more sophisticated evaluation procedures later on. The following is a description of the methods we have used to document the impact of our program. Keep in mind that these methods can be modified or combined with other approaches to meet the requirements of your organization.

The first step in evaluation is specifying the program's goals. Birth to Three has several interrelated goals: to provide information and support for parents, to prevent child abuse and neglect, and to strengthen families and neighborhoods. The underlying theme is that we are attempting to help parents get off to a good start during the first three years of child-rearing. The second step is developing ways to measure our progress toward achieving each goal. How elaborate the scheme becomes depends upon the resources you have and your need for precision.

For a Birth to Three program, evaluation assessments typically attempt to answer two questions: "How many families are served by our organization?" and "Does the program actually help them?" The answers will allow you or an outside observer to establish, for example, whether you are an organization that reaches very few people but has a significant impact on them, or an organization that has a modest impact on many people. Answering the first of these questions is fairly easy; answering the second is quite difficult.

Describing the services that you provide can be as simple as keeping a tally of the number of people contacted by each aspect of your program. If you want to know how effectively the organization is spending its resources, this will make it possible for you to assess the time and money going into each activity. You might discover, for example, that many people are calling to ask routine questions that could be answered in a newsletter or poster. This information is also quite useful for making budget projections and decisions regarding which services to cut and which to expand.

Determining whether you are actually helping parents is considerably more complex. Entire texts have been written on methods for evaluating social service programs. If you want to take a sophisticated approach, someone in the organization (or a consultant) will need to understand the elements of questionnaire design and statistical analysis. However, your efforts do not have to be elaborate to be of value. Our suggestion is, as usual, to begin with something simple that you can handle easily and add more sophisticated techniques as your program expands. Like most skills, program evaluation improves with experience.

We have used simple questionnaires as our primary means of evaluating whether or not we are helping families. Basically, the questionnaires ask parents about their goals in joining the organization and whether their needs have been met. Parents are also asked which Birth to Three services they have used and whether they would recommend Birth to Three to other parents. The answers to some of these questions can be obtained by tallying or averaging the responses of parents to the questionnaire. Other parts of the questionnaire are less structured and require individual reading to see what people think when they express themselves in their own words. Both types of information are useful.

The questionnaire that we have used for evaluation purposes is reproduced in Appendix 6.1. It can be used as a place to start in designing your own. Some of the results of our own periodic surveys of parents in our program have already been presented and discussed in the introduction to this book. These results suggest that most parents feel that the program is helping them to be better parents, and would recommend it to others.

Even though it is good to use the best methods you can afford, it is important to realize that even the most elaborate evaluation procedures cannot "prove" that some parents are more successful than others, much less that you have improved their parenting skills. To some extent, you need confidence that the theory behind the program is valid, so that if you are providing services to parents, you are accomplishing at least part of your goal. The theory behind Birth to Three is that providing support and information to parents will improve their childrearing skills and that these refinements in parenting skills will result in children who are healthier and more well-adjusted.

Current psychological research lends credibility to the Birth to Three model. There is growing evidence that social isolation or "insularity" increases the risk of child abuse and neglect. Insularity is a technical term for the quantity and quality of a mother's day-to-day contact with the world outside her home. Mothers who are relatively isolated and have disproportionately more unpleasant interactions with others during the day tend to be less effective as caretakers of their children. This diminished effectiveness, in turn, leads to less desirable child behavior, which itself creates more of the unpleasantness that impairs parenting skills. Even if the child-management skills are still there, they may not be implemented consistently. On the other hand, research suggests that positive social contacts can help buffer stresses (such as those related to having a new baby in the home). Thus, a program such as Birth to Three that teaches parenting skills and reduces isolation should reduce the risk of child abuse and neglect—even though hard evidence is difficult to come by.

Deriving conclusions about the effectiveness of prevention programs requires painstaking research. Shallow studies may be worse than none at all. It is tempting, for example, to measure the success of a child-abuse prevention program by looking for changes in the reported rate of child abuse. Yet, a successful program may actually increase that rate by increasing community awareness about the importance of reporting instances of abuse. Only after community awareness of the problem has peaked would the positive effects of a prevention program begin to show up as a decline in incidents reported.

Moreover, the statistics on child abuse never reveal the number of parents who felt pushed beyond their limit but did not quite lose control. At one time or another, most parents have felt infuriated with their child, although in calmer moments they may find it hard to imagine how their child could incite such anger. Even though it is not scientific data, there is something to be learned from the stories told by parents. A mother in one Birth to Three group called another member of her group one afternoon toward dinnertime to ask if she could bring her one-year-old over. "I can't take him anymore," she said, "this kid is driving me crazy—I think I'm going to kill him!" A few minutes later she arrived and deposited the baby, his blanket, and his bottle on the floor. As she left she said, "I'm going somewhere to sit—I'll be back in about an hour." The other mother was impressed by her candor—she had certainly known days like that herself. It was comforting to know that she could ask this friend to do the same thing for her the next time she felt that she was coming apart. It is important for parents to have somewhere to turn when they feel that they are at their wits' end. Having a "pressure-release valve" can make all the difference when it comes to keeping things from getting out of hand. The benefits of peer support seem self-evident without elaborate evaluation studies. A support network can make the difference between a parent who is competent but feels lonely, trapped, and resentful, and one who is equally competent and feels nurtured by a strong social framework.

Index to Chapter 7

CHAPTER 7

Discussion Outline for Eight Group Meetings

As we have said before, Birth to Three's purpose is to provide support and information to new parents. The parent meetings described in Chapter 4 are the vehicle for delivering this support. The second component, information, is developed in this chapter. In order to make it easier to offer parent support meetings and/or evening educational classes, we have included a detailed curriculum for eight two-hour discussions. Even if you have never been formally trained in child development, you should be able to use this curriculum successfully.

Each topic for discussion represents an important area of information for parents with infants. The group leader should read the material for each meeting before the scheduled meeting time and make arrangements for speakers well in advance. The material has been written so that it can be read out loud to the group to educate members and stimulate discussion directly (italics have been used to distinguish those parts that are meant only for the group leader). These materials have worked well for us. However, you can certainly adapt them to fit your own needs, expanding on some topics so that they last several sessions, changing the order of presentation, or adding and eliminating topics to make the discussions more pertinent to your group members. It is up to you as a group leader to determine the way to use this discussion outline. Inexpensive reprints of this section of the book entitled "Educational Materials for Birth to Three Groups" are also available from Castalia Publishing Company, Parent Education Division, P.O. Box 1587, Eugene, Oregon, 97440. Group members may want to purchase copies of this so that they can become familiar with the topics that are discussed at meetings. Parents may also want to purchase copies of this material for their own use.

Short feature articles, written by professionals, accompany the descriptive material for meetings #2–7. These articles have been included to provide more extensive background information on key topics from a slightly different perspective. There is also a list of suggested readings included for each meeting to help you find more information on a particular topic. In addition to these suggested readings and professional articles, an annotated reading list appears on page 257. Because Birth to Three does not endorse any one approach or orientation to parenting, the materials cited in the reading list have been selected to expose parents to several ways of looking at the issues. Two or three sentences have been written about each book to highlight what each of these resources has to offer. Think of this list as a good place to start looking for more information, but let your own preferences and opinions be your guide in selecting additional materials to help you learn about parenting.

These materials have been carefully selected to provide an overview of the issues that concern new parents. It should be noted, however, that some topics such as infant illnesses have been avoided because it is felt that these topics are not appropriate for group discussions. The issues involved are complex, and it is not a good idea to encourage parents to diagnose and/or provide treatment for infants who are experiencing medical problems. It is always better to refer questions about health to a physician or pediatrician.

Although the curriculum covers eight meetings, groups often continue to meet for more than eight weeks (some, in fact, have stayed together for five or six years). As the children grow, new topics for discussion continually arise. A list of additional topics that can be used to generate group discussions is provided in Appendix 7.1. You may want to read the list out loud so that as a group you can select the topics that are of most interest.

MEETING 1

The Challenge Facing New Parents

Goals

To introduce group members to Birth to Three and what it offers, give an overview of the topics that will be covered in coming sessions, and "break the ice" by encouraging each person to talk about her birth experience and what it feels like to be a new parent. The discussion can then be shifted to several related topics: the myth of the "ideal" parent, coping strategies for dealing with stress, selecting appropriate toys, and safety issues.

Introduce the Program

Preliminaries. First, hand out name tags and pass around a sheet of paper on which each person can write her name, address, telephone number, baby's name, and baby's birthdate. This list of group members can be duplicated and distributed at the next meeting. If the group is structured as a class, it would be a good idea to give everyone a list of the topics to be

103

covered during the coming sessions.

Explain, in your own words, the need for a program like Birth to Three. Babies can change our lives in many positive ways, and sometimes in distressing ways as well. Support from others who know what we are going through can buffer some of that stress and help restore our sense of well-being. Birth to Three is a program that promotes good parenting skills and positive attitudes toward childrearing. Our program does not endorse any one philosophy or approach to parenting—our intent is to act as a vehicle for information, not as a filter. We will cover a wide range of ideas and, in the process, we will try to educate ourselves and give support to each other.

Describe the other services offered by your organization. Even if you are not currently providing all the following services, you might read this list to give group members a feeling for what a full-scale Birth to Three program can offer: parenting classes (including special classes for teenage parents and other parents under particular stress), a newsletter, a telephone "warm line," and educational events such as lectures and panel discussions.

Show the Birth to Three poster. This is a directory of community services for parents with infants or small children. It has been set up as a poster so that you can hang it on the wall in your baby's room or near the phone. The books listed at the bottom of the poster are recommended readings that are available at the public library. Note the poison-control number—this is the number to call if you suspect that your child has swallowed a substance that could be harmful. In general, we suggest that you consult your doctor about any symptoms or behaviors that seem unusual for your child. Don't ever feel embarrassed about calling a physician to ask questions. Most doctors are more than willing to spend time answering simple questions in order to avoid discouraging parents from asking a question that may indicate something serious about their child's health.

If your organization is just starting up, a good first project is to survey the local resources and generate a Birth to Three poster for your community. Ask if there are members of the group who are interested in working on this project.

Show the newsletter. The Birth to Three newsletter is published in Eugene every other month. The newsletter contains articles about parenting and child development, book reviews, and listings of community events of interest to parents. *Ask the group if they are interested in subscribing to the newsletter—it is an excellent source of material for discussion.*

Discussion

Birth experiences. *After describing the Birth to Three organization, have group members introduce themselves and talk about their birth experiences. Ask for a volunteer to go first. The group leader should probably be last, unless no one else is willing to start.*

Questions for Discussion:

How was the delivery?
What was your reaction to seeing the baby?
What was your partner's reaction?
What did you expect having a baby would be like?
How does the reality compare with your
　expectations so far?

The Myth of the "Ideal" Parent

Show the group a copy of one of the popular parents' magazines, leafing through the ads and pointing out the mothers in the glossy pictures. Have the members of the group discuss how this image of motherhood compares with what they have experienced so far.

Questions for Discussion:

Is this the way you feel?

Do these pictures represent you?

How would you describe the ideal parent?

How do you compare with your ideal?

Many of us, especially with the first baby, feel pressured to live up to the baby magazine "mystique," to be a super-mom. Is it possible to do it all—be a good mother, housekeeper, cook, an alluring wife, and a career woman? Most of us quickly find out that these expectations are unrealistic. After giving birth, our bodies don't look or feel the way they used to. We may feel disturbed about the chaos in the house and find ourselves unable to rest until the place is clean. With little uninterrupted time to read or pursue our former interests, and no "news" to report to our partners beyond the baby's exploits, we may have the feeling at times that we have thrown our minds into the diaper pail along with everything else. During bleak moments, it may seem like the baby is developing while we are not. At first, most of us can barely struggle out of a dressing gown and into some clothes toward dinner time. All this can quickly erode a person's self-image.

Coping Strategies

Ask group members to describe some of the problems that they have encountered and the coping strategies that they have used. Parenting can be stressful, and both parents need to take good care of themselves to be able to nurture the baby. Try to get plenty of rest from the start; nap while the baby sleeps. Remember, things always look worse when you are tired. Force yourself to let the chores go. Think about what is more important—a clean sink, or a healthy, rested mother. Parenting won't always be as time-consuming as it is at the beginning. You won't always feel on-call 24 hours a day. Take a long-range view of things—the baby will only be small enough to hold and cuddle for a very short time. Meanwhile, make it a point to do some things for yourself whenever you can: go to a movie, read a book, play racquetball, etc. Taking time for yourself helps to improve your mood and keeps you in good spirits.

Even if preventive steps are taken, there will be times when one or both parents are tense and upset. What are some ways to deal with this situation? There are many different approaches to reducing stress and relaxing that seem to work for new parents. For example, you might call a friend to talk, ask a friend over to visit, or invite yourself over to a friend's house. Put the baby in the crib for 10 minutes so that you can read the paper and drink a cup of tea. Another possibility is to lay the baby down on the floor near you and do some quick exercises. Take a walk around the block with the baby in a stroller—just getting out of the house will often help to defuse a strained moment.

Ask the group to discuss how the transition to parenthood can be difficult for fathers as well as for mothers. Many fathers feel pushed aside, useless, and left out of the closeness between the mother and the baby. Mothers can help fathers take an active role by being encouraging and positive, and finding things for them to do with the baby. Try to remember that it is all right for fathers and mothers to relate differently to the baby—there is no one "right" way. Finally, it is very important to share your thoughts and feelings with your partner. Good communication is essential to working together as a team.

Appropriate Toys

Discuss the types of toys and activities that babies first enjoy. At about one month your baby will typically respond to your voice, your face, and to brightly colored and patterned objects. At this age, they are still too young for rattles. Keep in mind that it is easiest for babies to see objects that are eight to 24 inches away (12 to 24 inches is best). Singing simple songs and rhymes is an excellent way to entertain and soothe your baby; a few of the traditional songs and finger-plays are provided in Appendix 7.2. Experiment to find the sorts of games and activities that you and your baby both enjoy. Talk to your baby; hearing the sounds of language is the first step in language development. *(Note also that the topic of selecting appropriate toys will be discussed in more detail in Meeting #4).*

Safety Suggestions

> Never leave the baby unattended on a raised surface.
> When changing diapers, put the pins out of reach.
> Keep the floors and stairs in your house clear so that you don't fall with the baby.
> Use an approved car seat whenever the baby is in the car. You might try using the car seat around the house so that the baby becomes accustomed to it.

Summing Up the Discussion

Before bringing the discussion to an end, get some feedback from the group. Are there any other questions or issues that anyone would like to raise? Is the meeting time and place convenient for everybody? Does anyone need a ride to the meeting? Each person's contribution is important, and comments and suggestions are always welcome. Is there anyone in the group who has knowledge to share in an area such as language development or nutrition, or does anyone have access to a professional who might be an interesting speaker for the group (a doctor, nurse, family counselor, etc.)? In many ways, the input of group members determines how stimulating and rewarding the experience of belonging to this group will be.

Next week we'll talk about feeding, sleeping, and crying.

Suggested Readings for Meeting #1

Boston Children's Medical Center. *Child Health Encyclopedia.* Richard I. Feinbloom, M.D., Ed. New York: Dell, 1978.

Brazelton, T. Berry, M.D. *Infants and Mothers: Differences in Development.* New York: Dell, rev. ed., 1983.

Leach, Penelope. *Your Baby and Child: From Birth to Age Five.* New York: Knopf, 1978.

Princeton Center for Infancy. *The Parenting Advisor.* Frank Caplan, Ed. New York: Anchor, 1978.

MEETING 2

Sleeping, Feeding, and Crying

Goals

To provide background information and practical suggestions for dealing with three areas of baby activity on which so much of our attention as new parents is focused. Begin by exchanging stories about personal experiences, then add information from this discussion outline. The discussion should give parents an opportunity to help each other work out solutions to specific problems they may be encountering.

Preliminaries. Pass out name tags, the class roster, and the list of topics for forthcoming meetings. If a new mother has joined the group, have everyone introduce herself and her baby. Then go around the circle and invite each person to describe some of the things that happened during the past week (the group leader should be last).

111

Discussion

Sleeping Patterns

Have each member of the group discuss her baby's sleeping patterns. There are usually substantial differences in sleeping patterns from one baby to the next. Some infants quickly establish a regular sleeping pattern, but most newborn babies have a fairly erratic schedule, at least for a while. Adults operate on a 24-hour cycle, but some babies seem to follow an 18-or 36-hour cycle. Try to keep your expectations low and remember that an erratic sleeping schedule is not a sign of mismanagement on your part. The "standard" baby who sleeps for 20 hours a day, wakes up for feedings and then politely goes back to sleep, is a myth. Keeping a chart of your baby's sleeping/waking/crying cycles for a few days will help you to discover a pattern (see Appendix 7.3). Perhaps your baby is actually sleeping more than you thought, or crying less. In any case, the chart should be interesting to keep as a record of your baby's progress. You may also notice that changes in your baby's sleeping patterns are associated with developmental milestones such as teething, sitting up, rolling over, and walking. Illness will also affect the way your baby sleeps.

Getting some rest yourself. Ask the group to discuss some ways to make sure that parents get enough sleep. Being rested is so important to all aspects of parenting that napping during the day, unplugging the telephone, and putting a "Do not disturb" notice on your door are all strategies that you should consider. Ask friends or relatives to relieve you when you are desperate for sleep. Now is a perfect time to ask people for help; many of your friends would probably be delighted to make a meal for you, do some shopping, or take care of the baby for a while.

Questions for Discussion:

> What do you think about having the baby sleep in your room?/In your bed?
>
> When do you expect the baby to be able to sleep through the night?
>
> Does anyone have any other issues to raise in connection with babies' sleeping patterns, or any problems that they would like to bring up in the group?

Feeding

By now you've decided on either breast or bottle feeding, or perhaps you're doing a combination of both. Regardless of the type of feeding you have chosen, remember that the closeness of your body and the look in your eyes are nourishment to the baby too.

Questions for Discussion:

> Have you encountered any feeding problems?
>
> Have you worked out how often and how much to feed the baby?
>
> Have you had to deal with pressure from family members or friends concerning breast versus bottle feeding? Have you been able to resolve these pressures?
>
> Are there any other questions about feeding?

Crying

Ask group members how they cope with a crying baby. Babies always cry for a reason: because they are wet, hungry, sleepy, uncomfortable, or just want to be held. If you routinely let your newborn cry it out for long periods of time (for example, 10 minutes or more) you may be communicating that the world is not a comforting, trustworthy place.

Questions for Discussion:

What are some good ways to calm a fussy baby?

Are there times when you should let your baby cry it out, and at what age do you start doing this?

How do you deal with crying in the middle of the night?

What are some ways to manage your own feelings when you are faced with an infant who won't stop crying?

Infant Health

Questions regarding infant health are likely to be asked at group meetings. However, many of the issues involved are complex and beyond the scope of this book and the expertise of lay group leaders (mention some of the books listed under "Medical Guides" and "Basic Health and Child Development" in the annotated reading list). Stress again the importance of having a pediatrician that you can call if you have questions or concerns about your infant's health. Remind group members that this is the time to arrange for babies' immunizations, if they haven't already done so.

Summing Up the Discussion

The concerns of new parents are primarily centered around the sleeping, feeding, and crying behavior of their newborns. It is for this reason that the discussion of our first meeting has been focused on these issues. We hope that some of your questions have been answered, and that by exchanging experiences, you have some idea about what other parents are going through with their newborns. The first several months can be exhausting as well as richly satisfying. Babies usually don't establish regular patterns of sleeping, feeding, and crying right away. There is a lot of adjusting and accommodating necessary on all sides before routines are established.

Next week we'll be talking about individual differences and stages of development through eight months.

Suggested Readings for Meeting #2

Cheldelin, Larry V., M.D. *Your Baby's Secret World*. Brookline Village, Mass.: Brandon Press, 1983.

Rozdilsky, Mary Lou and Banet, Barbara. "Coping with a Crying Baby," in *What Now? A Handbook for New Parents*. New York: Scribner, 1975.

Preventative Child Care

BRUCE STRIMLING, M.D., F.A.A.P.

Women's and Children's Clinic
Eugene, Oregon

Even healthy babies need to be taken to a pediatrician on a regular basis. Whether you call it "well baby" care, health maintenance, or health supervision, visits to your baby's doctor over the course of his or her childhood can improve the quality of your child's health, enhance the enjoyment that you derive from childrearing, and actually save you money. The fragmentation of the extended family and the mobility of young families with children have made it more important than ever to establish an ongoing relationship with a child health care provider. Regular visits to your baby's doctor make it possible to diagnose physical and emotional health problems before they become severe, and provide an opportunity for parents to receive preventative counseling. Most of our childrearing practices are based on folk culture or fable. As these practices are exposed to scientific investigation, many turn out to be substantiated and worthwhile. Others turn out to be "old wives' tales" that are unfounded and may lead to unnecessary anxiety or busy work that wastes the parents' time and money. It is important to keep in mind that the field of child health is a rapidly advancing discipline, and a problem which had no treatment a year ago may now be easily and effectively treated. For these reasons, only routinely scheduled periodic examinations can afford your family the maximum benefits of modern health care.

Although a routine physical is an important component of each visit, the baby's doctor does a great deal more than this when you bring your child in for a health-supervision contact. The visits should also include an assessment of hearing, speech, eyesight, and blood pressure at appropriate ages. Special attention is given to evaluating the child's growth, and appropriate weights and measurements are noted (during infancy, measuring the head circumference is part of the examination). A direct or indirect assessment of each child's intellectual, motor, and emotional development should also be included. In addition, the physician should assess the parents' childrearing skills so that special assistance or referral can be provided to those families who need help in this area. During the physical, or after it has been completed, the physician can answer questions that parents typically have regarding all aspects of childrearing. The doctor should encourage parents to keep a list of questions to be answered during routine office visits.

Another very important component of the health maintenance visit is referred to by physicians as anticipatory guidance or parent education. Most physicians consider this aspect of the visit much more important than the physical checkup and many doctors modify or shorten examinations during some visits to give themselves time to deal with important educational issues. It is at this time that the physician discusses topics such as preventing accidents and poisoning, what to expect in terms of behavioral problems and how to deal with them, nutrition, toilet training, use and abuse of tel-

117

evision, immunization, and many other subjects. These are things that parents need to know about in order to insure that their child will be as healthy and emotionally secure as possible. The visit generally ends with the child receiving the appropriate immunizations and laboratory tests and the next routine visit is scheduled. If abnormalities have been discovered, treatments may be planned or started, or a referral to a specialist may be made.

Printed materials (handouts) regarding common health problems are generally made available to parents. This is a help for parents who cannot remember everything they have been told in the office. Often, extra reading will be recommended for parents who are interested in learning more about a specific illness or aspect of child health. Finally, complete and updated health records should always be kept on every child. This information, which no parent can be expected to remember years later (particularly if there are several children), often proves to be critically important if the child has health problems later on in life. Your childhood medical history can have a bearing on problems that are experienced by your offspring. It is perfectly acceptable to ask to see your child's chart as this is an important legal record that you should be familiar with.

Parents sometimes naively and incorrectly assume that since their child has been in the doctor's office several times in the last year with illnesses it is not necessary to bring the child in for the next recommended health-supervision visit. This sometimes turns out to be a tragic error. When a sick child is brought to the physician, the doctor concentrates on the system or systems involved in the illness. Under these circumstances, where time is limited and there is a problem that must be dealt with, even relatively obvious abnormalities in other systems may go unnoticed. Because of the rapid changes that take place in children's bodies, early detection and treatment of abnormalities is critical.

An often unrecognized benefit of regular health-maintenance visits is the relationship that develops between the doctor and the family. Since children are usually feeling well when they come in, and most doctors enjoy doing these examinations, it can be fun for everyone involved. The time spent together during these visits promotes a better understanding between physician and patient and contributes to the development of a strong personal relationship. This "caring" doctor-patient relationship is beneficial to both the physician and the family. A sick and frightened preschool child who is seeing a doctor for the first time will be less cooperative (or perhaps frankly uncooperative), making it impossible for the physician to be sensitive to subtle symptoms or findings. One of the pediatrician's greatest nightmares is trying to examine the abdomen of a frightened, uncomfortable, and uncooperative three-year-old child who may have appendicitis. Not being able to do a thorough exam sometimes leads to unnecessary surgery or, worse yet, a missed appendicitis that goes on to complications.

One of the greatest obstacles to a child receiving the preventative care that is necessary and recommended is the cost. Some parents hate to spend discretionary funds on preventative care for a child who seems basically healthy; yet there is clear evidence that preventative care for children saves money in the long run. There have been a number of studies of large federally funded programs that indicate that the cost of providing medical services for children who have received preventative care is significantly less than the cost for children receiving only episodic sick care. This savings is directly related to the fact that children receiving preventative care are less likely to be hospitalized. There seems to be little awareness of the fact that on the average, one day in the hospital costs more than all of the preventative care recommended for a child from birth through age 21, including all immunizations and appropriate laboratory determinations. There are a number of insurance programs which now include preventative health care for children as one of their benefits. Families with children should choose this sort of insurance if it is available to them. If not, parents should put pressure on their employers, unions, and insurance companies to see that this coverage is provided. Since preventative care is inexpensive compared to the other services that insurance pays for, the cost of adding preventative care is typically $2 to $3 per month per policy (according to data gathered by the American Academy of Pediatrics, 1985).

The recommended frequency of preventative health visits varies from physician to physician, and some doctors may alter their recommendations depending on the circumstances of the child or family. Certain high-risk individuals need to be seen more frequently. Generally, every newborn baby needs to be thoroughly examined by a physician, and then re-examined two to three weeks later to make sure that the baby has successfully made the transition from intrauterine to extra-uterine life. Following this, visits tend to be quite frequent in the first six to 12 months of life and progressively less frequent following that. The American Academy of Pediatrics recommends visits at 2 weeks, 2 months, 4 months, 6 months, 9 months, 1 year, 15 months, 18 months, 2 years, 3 years, 4 years, and 5 years of age. You can see that the sequence changes from every other month, to every third month, to every six months, and finally to once a year. Children grow most rapidly and go through the most changes when they are younger, and then become progressively more stable as they grow older. In addition, mothers and fathers become better parents with time and do not require as much supervision and help as they settle into their new roles.

When you choose a physician for your baby-to-be, be sure you choose one with a strong commitment to preventative care. Although the benefits are well documented, if the doctor does not personally feel that preventative care is important to the well-being of your child, you can be sure that very little time will be spent on preventative care.

In addition to being competent, your baby's physician must be available when the need arises. Above all, your child's doctor should be someone who is easy to communicate with; he or she should be open and responsive to your concerns, questions, and complaints. You must know what your pediatrician expects of you, and your doctor should know what you expect as well. If you are dissatisfied, it is a good idea to interview several other physicians until you find someone who you think you will prefer. If you have gone through two or three physicians who have been carefully chosen but find that you are dissatisfied anyway, consider the possibility that your expectations may be unrealistic.

Regular preventative health care for your child is certainly worth the time, energy, and money that is involved. It will augment your child's physical well-being and increase the enjoyment and fulfillment that you experience as parents. In addition, it brings one more caring and loving person into your child's life and provides a valuable lifetime resource for your child's health.

Recommended Readings

Boston Children's Medical Center. *Child Health Encyclopedia*. Richard I. Feinbloom, M.D., Ed. New York: Dell, 1978.

Brazelton, T. Berry, M.D. *Infants and Mothers: Differences in Development*. New York: Dell, rev. ed., 1983.

Meadowbrook Medical Reference Group. *The Parent's Guide to Baby and Child Medical Care*. Terril H. Hart, M.D., Ed. Deephaven, Minn.: Meadowbrook Press, 1982.

MEETING 3

Individual Differences and Stages of Development through Eight Months

Goals

To talk about infant temperament, the different stages of development from birth to eight months, and what we can do as parents to facilitate development.

Preliminaries. *Begin the meeting with some personal discussion. If the topic has not come up yet, you might ask each person to describe what she did before the baby was born. If this has already been talked about, then just ask each person to share news about how things have been going lately.*

Discussion

Individual Differences

To get the discussion going, ask each mother to describe her baby in terms of overall activity level and mood; some

123

other dimensions to consider are curiosity, regularity, adaptability, and sensory threshold. We have all observed that normal babies differ from each other in many ways. Observe your baby carefully and try to discover the patterns in his or her behavior; experiment to find the best way to interact with your baby. Even within the same family the personality that distinguishes each baby is unique; what worked for one baby may not be right for the next.

If you have a newborn who seems unsettled or cries a lot of the time, don't blame yourself—it's not a reflection on you. Ask other parents in your Birth to Three group to suggest some ways to soothe your baby. Call your pediatrician for advice (perhaps there is a physical problem). Above all, resist the temptation to hold it against the baby. Remember, there are no "good" or "bad" babies. Your infant does not intend to make life miserable for you. Like parents, babies are only doing the best they can under the circumstances.

Stages of Development

Since many first-time parents are relatively unfamiliar with developmental stages, it may be a good idea to present the following material before trying to generate group discussion. Ask parents what progress they have noticed in their infant's development. These developmental stages should be viewed as a general description of babies at a particular age. Individual babies within the normal range may vary considerably with respect to the age at which they acquire a specific skill. Babies are often more advanced in one area than another, and sometimes it seems that they concentrate on mastering one thing at a time. Be patient—even though early achievements seem very important at the time, in the long run the developmental timing of each new skill does not make a lot of difference (nor is it predictive of later development). Rather than attempting to "push" your baby from one stage to the

124

next, try to enjoy to the fullest each stage that your baby passes through.

The First Six Weeks

Typical behaviors at this age include: rooting, sucking, grasping, and glancing, all of which are components of early intelligence. Babies are interested in faces and your face and voice are probably your baby's most entertaining toys. At this stage babies tend to be sensitive to abrupt stimulation, such as loud noises and bright lights, and they change moods rapidly.

Activities. Knowing what babies are capable of doing can help you to make them happy. At this age babies can already discriminate a wide range of sounds. Imitate the sounds your baby makes to see if you can get a "conversation" going. Music boxes and other musical toys are appealing, and so are songs and the sound of your voice.

When babies are on their backs they look to the side most of the time and so mobiles or other displays placed to the side rather than directly overhead will probably get the most attention. Tracking a slowly moving object is a good game for babies at this age. Move an object back and forth (vertically or horizontally) eight inches or so above your baby's head and watch the baby follow it visually. You should also put the baby in a variety of positions and provide things to look at (try to imagine what it would be like to depend on someone to move you).

Some other appropriate activities for this age are rocking, bathing, walking the baby around the house (pointing out the colored and patterned things that hang on the walls), and simple baby exercises. Try lifting the baby's hands up, then across his or her chest, or move the baby's legs as though he or she were riding a bicycle. Do the exercises slowly and don't force the movements. Both you and the baby should be relaxed and having fun.

125

Six Weeks to Three-and-a-Half Months

At this stage babies are more awake and alert than before. They smile regularly and spend a lot of time studying their hands. Their fingers are more relaxed now and are tightened into a fist less often. They are beginning to be able to grasp objects placed in their hands (a few seconds at a time at first), and at about two-and-a-half months will start putting objects into their mouths to explore them. They are also beginning to swipe and bat at objects. Mobiles that were entertaining when the baby was younger may no longer be appropriate or safe and should be removed. At this age, babies are very sociable, and are even more interested in human faces. They are beginning to respond to sound by turning to the source. By three-and-a-half months babies have nearly mature visual capabilities. They can look at objects held in their hands for a few seconds and may sometimes pass an object from one hand to another at midline. They can visually track smaller objects, and the tracking is not so automatic.

Activities. Try putting the baby, stomach down, on a mat or blanket on the floor for a while every day (five minutes or so at a time) with some toys close by for the baby to look at. At this age babies like mirrors and crib toys that can be swiped at, and the old favorites—cuddling and talking.

Three-and-a-Half Months to Five-and-a-Half Months

Babies are very congenial at this age and it is a great time for photographing. They are discovering their feet, rolling over from back to front, and holding their heads up to look around. You may notice that the baby is beginning to reach deliberately for objects. Reaching is a complicated skill. The baby sees an object, moves a hand toward it, opens and closes his or her fingers to grasp it, and then may move the object to see it in a different position or bring it to the mouth to gum it. All this takes a lot of practice. At this stage you may observe the baby watching as he or she rotates a wrist, which is also an interesting exercise. The baby is beginning to understand that the hand and the object it holds are the same regardless of the viewing angle.

Activities. Talking to your baby while feeding, changing, and playing helps the baby associate the sound of your voice and your appearance with comfort and pleasure. Use simple language but expand it with repetition. "Diaper pin, I'm using a diaper pin to fasten your diaper."

Play games that involve naming body parts. Attach a balloon to your baby's wrist or ankle so that he or she can watch its movement—but don't try this without supervising. Grasp the baby's hands and let the baby pull to a sitting or standing position. Never lift the baby off the ground this way, though, as this could dislocate a shoulder.

Five-and-a-Half to Eight Months

This stage often marks the transition from the pre-crawling stage to full-fledged crawling. During the pre-crawling phase, the baby is sitting up and can take in, at least visually, more of the surroundings, but is frustrated by not being able to get to all those objects that look so attractive. Fine-motor coordination continues to improve and babies are fascinated by small things. The next few months are definitely a good time to keep your floors swept, and you should be wary of small objects that could result in choking. Do provide small things for exploration, but don't leave the baby unattended.

Babies are often crawling by the end of this stage. Make things easy on yourself and child-proof the house. Put safety latches on drawers and cabinets that are off limits and put all dangerous or valuable objects far from the baby's reach. Use gates to block stairways, up and down. Keep the doors to bathrooms and siblings' rooms closed—these areas are difficult to child-proof completely. Don't forget to put safety plugs in electric sockets. Babies do not have the intellectual capacity yet (and will not for at least another year) to restrain themselves from exploring the stereo, lamp cords, and other things that are supposed to be off limits. Saying "No!" will not help at this age, so it is easier on everyone to remove as many of these temptations as possible from the baby's reach.

Babies are beginning to be suspicious of strangers now. Be ready to tell friends that the baby's reaction is nothing personal. It's their unfamiliarity, not their personality, that makes the baby wary.

Activities. Cause and effect games are interesting for babies at this age—they love to throw and bang objects to see what happens. Light switches, hinged doors, and jack-in-the-boxes are good entertainment. Object permanence is developing—watch what happens when the baby is sitting in a high chair and drops a spoon over the side. Does he or she look over the tray to see where it fell?

Summing Up the Discussion

Think of the home as your child's learning laboratory. Put toys and decorations at your baby's level. Crawl around on the floor every now and then to see the area as your child does. Give your baby pots and pans, brushes, magazines you don't care about anymore, and containers for stacking and stuffing. Let babies feel the grass, pet animals, and touch the concrete—it's all very exciting to them.

Next week we'll be talking about play and language development.

Suggested Readings for Meeting #3

Levy, Janine. *The Baby Exercise Book: For the First Fifteen Months*. New York: Pantheon Books, 1975.

Painter, Genevieve. *Teach Your Baby*. New York: Simon & Schuster, 1971.

Princeton Center for Infancy and Early Childhood. *The First Twelve Months of Life: Your Baby's Growth Month by Month*. Frank Caplan, Ed. New York: Grosset & Dunlap, 1973.

White, Burton L. *The First Three Years of Life*. New York: Avon, 1975.

Developmental Stages: Birth to Eight Months

DIANE BRICKER, PH.D., AND SARAH GUMERLOCK, M.S.

Center on Human Development
University of Oregon
Eugene, Oregon

As parents, we are keenly interested in how our babies grow and develop. After a baby is born, if all goes well, parents usually are excited, pleased, proud, and naturally a little apprehensive. Most parents worry about their baby developing without problems. Will their baby be attractive, happy and loveable? Will their child have friends and manage in school without serious problems? The concerns that parents have about the developmental progress of their children are created in part by the widely publicized belief that what happens to infants during their first several years of life is an important factor in determining later growth and development.

This article describes some of the major developmental changes that take place between birth and the age of eight months. To assist parents in focusing their attention on the critical aspects of infant behavior, we have suggested that they observe their babies under a variety of conditions. The information gained from these observations will help parents to understand and appreciate what infants can and cannot do as they move through the early stages of development.

During the first eight months, infants spend most of their waking time learning about their physical and social environments. Babies are not born knowing that balls are for bouncing, chairs are for sitting in, and spoons are for eating with. Infants must learn the fundamental properties of things through systematic interactions with people and the physical objects that surround them. As infants become more experienced, they gradually learn that objects can be distinguished from people, and that people differ from each other. Infants must learn about the social functions people perform, and understand which of their own behaviors are acceptable and which are not. These subtle social skills are taught to infants by parents as they interact with their babies. This is part of the basic learning process by which infants move from caring only about themselves to understanding the feelings and needs of others.

Birth to Two Months

During the early period after birth, the first major task confronting infants is the behavioral and psychological adjustment to life outside the womb. Some infants adjust easily, while others appear to adapt slowly to the variations presented by their new air environment. Even before birth, infants are learning about their world. Shortly after birth, infants have the ability to look, listen and feel. Even more astounding is that infants are able to learn from these early sensory experiences. As parents, it is important to remember that your child is literally learning all the time.

If you watch your baby carefully during the first weeks of life, you will discover that he or she is surprisingly able to respond and learn about various sensory stimuli. Try making a noise (like ringing a bell or banging a spoon) while your baby cannot see you. Observe your infant's behavior. Did he or she become quiet and look around, or did the noise make the baby wave and kick? Either type of response is an indication that the infant has heard the sound. Infants appear to be able to hear the same range of sounds as adults. The task for infants as they grow older is to learn to attach specific meanings to the wide variety of sounds around them.

Your baby will respond to visual and tactile stimulation in a similar fashion. For example, try moving a large colorful object into the infant's line of sight (about eight to 10 inches in front of his or her eyes). Move the object gently to attract his or her attention and then watch your infant's eyes explore the object. Gently stroking your baby's cheek should also produce a response (typically, the baby will become quiet and turn his or her mouth toward the stroking). These responses to auditory, visual, and tactile stimulation indicate that their senses are ready to receive information and they are beginning to learn about their physical and social environments. However, infants have poor motor control during this early period, and thus must wait for things to happen to them (or for them) in order for this learning to take place.

Two to Four Months

The process of socialization begins during the second two-month period. During this stage, if you place your face close to your baby's and say, "Hi, baby," what response do you notice? Typically, he or she will become quiet, watch your face intently, and then squirm or coo in apparent delight. If you continue to talk to your baby and perhaps tickle his or her tummy, you may be able to detect some early signs that your baby is participating in this social activity. By now you have become very important to your baby, and one of his or her greatest joys is "communicating" with you. You may also notice that after a few minutes of social stimulation, your baby will look away or turn his or her head. Your infant needs to withdraw momentarily to "recover." If you wait quietly, your

132

baby will turn toward you when he or she is ready for another communicative interaction.

Observe what your baby does when lying on his or her back. Usually, when babies are awake and alert, they will be moving their arms and legs. Sometimes the movements are small, and at other times they are more vigorous. Although the baby's arm and leg movements are still uncoordinated, there is better control now than there was during the first couple of weeks. Place your hands on your baby's feet and gently push his or her legs, bending the knees. If you gently push and extend the legs a few times, you may feel that your infant is beginning to understand the "game" and will participate by bending and pushing in response to your rhythm.

During this developmental period, most infants cannot grab toys; however, if you hold a rattle in front of your baby, you will notice that he or she will attempt to reach out and touch or grasp the toy. The baby will swipe or swing at the object because the lack of motor control prohibits a more controlled reaching response.

When infants are two to four months of age they still lack sufficient control over body movements to permit active exploration. However, they are beginning to have some control over their social environment by developing some rudimentary social skills such as smiling and actively reacting to you in other ways. If you doubt this, try to walk past your baby without responding in some fashion when he or she is smiling at you.

Four to Six Months

This is an exciting time for infants and parents! Most infants can sit up with support for considerable periods of time. The upright position gives them a different view of the world and makes it easier for them to reach and grasp. Another new development that you might notice is that infants are now able to grab a toy or rattle when it is held out to them. Of course, at this age babies still have trouble trying to pick up small or large objects. In addition, you may notice that once your infant has grasped an object, he or she doesn't seem to be able to let go of it. Rather, things seem to fall from the infant's hand after he or she loses interest in them. You will also notice that hands, fingers, and feet are put into the mouth frequently and with ease.

By the age of six months most infants have acquired a lot of different sounds. If you listen to the sounds your baby makes, you will probably notice that some of the sounds are difficult for you to imitate. Other sounds are similar to those that make up the English language; these sounds are relatively easy to imitate.

Babies are good communicators by now. Although they do not have words, they can tell you when they feel good, when they are uncomfortable, when they want something that is within sight, and what they like and don't like to eat. Many people think that babies don't communicate until they can produce words, but if you observe your infant's cries, vocalizations, and gestures it will be clear to you that even at this age, your infant is a good communicator.

It is during this period that infants acquire the necessary motor control to move from being a passive observer to an initiator and explorer of the social and physical environments that are within reach. In addition, babies learn a variety of social skills that permit them to attract your attention and direct your activities. Finally, infants have become intrigued with attempting to recreate interesting happenings, so that you might observe your baby shaking an object or repeating other actions in an apparent attempt to duplicate a noise or movement.

Six to Eight Months

By this period, instead of being passive participants, infants begin to actively engage in many of the activities that make up their day. Babies no longer have to wait for someone to bring them an out-of-reach toy. By scooting, creeping, or rolling infants are now mobile and can get around enough to retrieve many desired objects. In addition, infants have learned to manipulate the objects that they find in a variety of ways to stimulate themselves. If you watch them playing with objects, you will notice that they are good at banging, shaking, tearing, patting, and so on. By trying these various actions with objects, babies learn about the properties of their physical world—that is, some things are good for throwing but not for sitting on, other objects are good for banging but not for rolling.

Offer your infant a series of novel or unfamiliar objects and watch how he or she uses different action schemes to discover how these new objects "work." Babies at this stage of development cannot learn about the world or solve problems in abstract ways (for example, by thinking about them). Infants must play with toys and objects directly to understand their properties.

Trying some other activities will help you discover some of the problems that your infants still cannot solve. For example, if you cover a toy that the baby is reaching for, the infant will stop reaching for it. If they can no longer see the toy, it ceases to exist for them. So, although infants have acquired many skills, they still lack many basic concepts about their world.

During this period, most infants begin to babble, repeating sequences of sounds such as "Mama" or "Dada." In a few months, this babbling will be refined into the infant's first words. Babies are good at imitating the sounds that they can make. For example, after your infant says "Mama," repeat the sounds. Typically, the baby will respond by saying "Mama" or will produce similar sounds. You can engage in chains of responses with your baby if you continue to imitate the sounds your baby produces.

135

Participating in nursery games is great fun for infants because they are now more active. Your baby may even begin to anticipate the next action, which tells you that he or she is starting to remember the game. Your infant may also cry or reach for a cookie before he or she has actually had a bite of it. Such actions by your infant are clear signs of mental growth. Your infant is beginning to recognize objects, people, and activities and remember their function without having to actually reproduce the activity.

A number of important developmental events occur for most infants during this period. The infant appears to be making sense out of the many objects and activities that are experienced on a daily basis. It is during this period that many infants develop the ability to recognize their parents and start to be wary of other people. Finally, the infant's physical abilities are expanding and the stage is being set for learning to walk and manipulate most environmental objects.

Summary

Many significant changes take place in infants during the first eight months of development. They make the transition from being a tiny bundle of uncoordinated responses that is completely dependent upon the outside world, to having a set of coordinated responses and a basic understanding about how the world functions. By eight months of age, they are actively exploring their surroundings and communicating with the people around them. They learn to distinguish their parents from everyone else, and begin to say "Mama" and "Dada" without being prompted. It is a very satisfying experience to watch your newborn baby pass through these stages of development. Parents who appreciate the changes in their babies will facilitate development naturally—this is one of the most important things that we can do for our children.

Again, a note of caution. The general developmental pattern outlined in this article reflects how most infants progress during the first eight months. It is extremely important to remember that your infant may or may not do all of the described responses. Some infants do not roll, some do not crawl, others babble very little, and some never become wary of strangers. This does not mean that something is wrong with your infant; rather, it indicates that infants are as individual as adults. Consequently, if your infant does not engage in some expected behaviors, but he or she seems happy and alert, there is probably nothing for you to worry about.

Recommended Readings

Brazelton, T. Berry, M.D. *Infants and Mothers: Differences in Development.* New York: Dell, rev. ed., 1983.

Chase, Richard A., Fisher, J.J. and Rubin, R.R. (Eds.). *Your Baby: The First Wondrous Year.* New York: Collier Books, 1984.

Gordon, Ira. J. *Baby Learning Through Baby Play: A Parent's Guide for the First Two Years.* New York: St. Martin's Press, 1970.

Gordon, Ira J. *Baby to Parent, Parent to Baby: A Guide to Developing Parent-Child Interaction in the First Twelve Months.* New York: St. Martin's Press, 1977.

Hagstrom, Julie and Morrill, Joan. *Games Babies Play and More Games Babies Play: A Handbook of Games to Play With Infants.* New York: Pocket Books, 1981.

Levy, Janine. *The Baby Exercise Book: For the First Fifteen Months.* New York: Pantheon Books, 1975.

Painter, Genevieve. *Teach Your Baby.* New York: Simon & Schuster, 1971.

Princeton Center for Infancy and Early Childhood. *The First Twelve Months of Life: Your Baby's Growth Month by Month.* Frank Caplan, Ed. New York: Grosset & Dunlap, 1973.

DEVELOPMENTAL CHART*
Birth to 8 months

Birth to 1 month

Area of Development	Skills
Fine Motor	• Moves arms randomly • Drops objects placed in hand • Keeps hands clenched into a fist • Regards objects momentarily
Gross Motor	• Reflexive movement
Social	• Smiles; produces comfort and distress sounds
Cognitive	• Orients to light and sound
Language	• Makes sounds • Responds to sound

2 months to 4 months	
Area of Development	**Skills**
Fine Motor	• Holds objects in middle of palm
	• Reaches for objects
Gross Motor	• Rolls from back to side
	• Plays with feet
	• Holds head steady
Social	• Smiles at "peekaboo"
	• Recognizes mother
	• Enjoys games
	• Smiles at self in mirror
Cognitive	• Follows slow moving object
	• Mouths objects
	• Grasps toys
	• Repeats interesting games
Language	• Makes vowels ("a," "e")
	• Begins babbling

4 months to 6 months

Area of Development	Skills
Fine Motor	• Transfers objects from one hand to the other hand • Turns to look at falling object that makes a lot of noise
Gross Motor	• Holds self up with arms • Lifts head • Rolls from back to stomach and from stomach to back
Self-Care	• Eats solids • Holds bottle while drinking • Cooperates in dressing
Social	• Stops crying when talked to • Vocalizes to initiate socializing • Watches faces
Cognitive	• Looks for objects that are partly hidden
Language	• Babbles

6 months to 8 months	
Area of Development	**Skills**
Fine Motor	• Bangs objects together
	• Watches mother move around room
	• Lets go of objects purposefully
Gross Motor	• Stands briefly
	• Crawls
Self-Care	• Holds bottle while drinking
	• Eats solids
	• Cooperates in dressing
Social	• Turns when name is called
	• Vocalizes to gain attention
	• Knows familiar people from strangers
	• Plays "peekaboo," "bye-bye," and ball games
Cognitive	• Waves and bangs objects
	• Searches for objects partly hidden
Language	• Babbles and uses gestures to communicate
	• Responds to some familiar words

*These data were taken in part from Cohen, M., & Gross, P. *The Developmental Resource: Behavioral Sequences for Assessment and Program Planning.* New York: Grune & Stratton, 1979. Reprinted by permission.

MEETING 4

Play, Toys, and Language Development

Goals

To expand our understanding of how babies learn through playing, using toys, and experimenting with language. Emphasis will be placed on pointing out ways for parents to "tie into" the learning process so that it is fun for both the parent and the baby.

Preliminaries. *Begin by taking a few minutes to share everyone's news. Ask the members of the group to think back to their earliest memories of childhood. What were some of their favorite games or things to do? Do they still have any of the toys that were special to them as a child?*

Discussion

Play

Start with some general questions about the purpose of play. What is play? Why is it important for babies? What do babies learn from playing? Babies' play has a purpose beyond having a good time. During play activities babies learn to use their eyes, ears, noses, hands, mouths, and their whole bodies. They also learn how the world works and how they can have an impact on it. They learn by trial and error, imitation, and by observing natural consequences. Each developmental stage is accompanied by new kinds of play as babies practice what they are learning.

Parents are their babies' first teachers and the home is the child's first learning environment. Play helps parents and babies develop a positive relationship. One way to put this in perspective is to think about how your parents and teachers helped you learn things as a child. What do you remember about your most and least favorite teachers? Favorite ones probably showed confidence in you and presented material in ways that made learning fun. We, as parents, can do the same for our children.

Babies enjoy both active and quiet play. Use quiet activities to calm your baby before bedtime. Don't wake the baby in order to play, or wait until a baby is tired to engage in active play. Initially, babies can entertain themselves for only short periods of time; don't expect your baby to play alone very much. If babies are entertaining themselves, leave them alone for a while—try to maintain a balance between interacting with the baby and encouraging independence. Spend good, focused time playing with the baby when he or she is ready to play with you. Then you won't need to feel guilty about taking time for yourself or for household chores.

Toys

Ask the group about the types of toys that their babies enjoy. Toys do not necessarily have to be expensive to be fun for babies. Household items are great toys: measuring spoons, plastic containers with lids and something inside for shaking, plastic cups, canning rings on a string, and so on. When buying toys, use the recommended age range as a guideline, but consider your own baby's abilities and interests as well. Be on the lookout for small parts, sharp points, and loud noises that might be frightening.

Young babies like to look at anything that resembles a human face or has sharp contrasts. For example, targets and other patterns with concentric circles interest them, while distorted faces do not. As they learn to reach, babies like sturdy mobiles about 12 inches above their eyes that they can touch. At about three months, babies watch their hands a lot and begin to put things into their mouths. Put only soft toys in their cribs, especially when the baby is practicing sitting up (and still toppling over). At about seven or eight months they start pulling things toward them and experimenting with cause and effect. Banging, dropping, and hiding things are fun at this stage, as are "peekaboo," "this little piggy," and "pat-a-cake."

Language Development

Ask the group to discuss how babies learn to talk. When do babies first begin to express themselves? What can parents do to help them learn? Language development is a complicated process that takes place in many small steps. The ability to *produce* language comes only after much experience. However, babies can understand what is being said to them long before they can talk. If you have tried to learn a foreign language, you have probably noticed that it is much easier to understand what is being said to you than it is to say something. Babies listen to words but they also pay attention to tone of voice and facial expression. As a result, speaking with gestures is an effective way to communicate. When you say "come here" and stretch out your hands, the words are only part of the message.

Use simple language, be repetitive, and emphasize important words. Speak slowly and clearly. Use eye contact and imitate the sounds that the baby makes. This will encourage

147

the baby to imitate the sounds that you make. Talk to the baby while feeding, changing diapers, and so on—tell the baby what you're doing. If you are doing something that gives the baby pleasure, he or she will associate the sound of your voice with that good feeling. Later on, use puppets and tell stories to your baby. Cut up old magazines to make scrapbooks of pictures your child can recognize and name. Finger plays and simple songs are also fun for babies (see Appendix 7.2).

Reading to your baby will also encourage language development. Begin reading to your baby when he or she is quite young so that both of you get into the habit. Start with simple books, one picture to a page, and talk about what is happening in the pictures. For young babies, use soft cloth or plastic books, then go on to thicker cardboard books. With practice, the baby will be able to flip the stiff pages alone at around one year of age. Use the library to find books of a higher quality than those that can be bought at the grocery store (this also saves you the expense of purchasing them).

Summing Up the Discussion

The first few years are a period of rapid learning and development. Sometimes, when you are with your baby day after day, it may not seem like any changes are taking place. However, each day provides a new set of lessons for your baby—by being sensitive to the things that interest your baby at each stage of development you can share some of the excitement as he or she discovers the world.

Next week we'll talk about the impact that babies have on their parents' relationship.

Suggested Readings for Meeting #4

Burtt, Kent Garland and Kalkstein, Karen. *Smart Toys*. New York: Harper Colophon, 1981.

Developmental Language and Speech Center. *Teach Your Child to Talk*. Grand Rapids, Michigan: CEBCO Standard Pub., 1975.

Marzollo, Jean. *Supertot*. New York: Harper Colophon, 1977.

Marzollo, Jean and Lloyd, Janice. *Learning Through Play*. New York: Harper Colophon, 1972.

Playing with Your Child

CAROLYN WEBSTER-STRATTON, PH.D.

Associate Professor and Director
Pediatric Nurse Practitioner Program
University of Washington
Seattle, Washington

There is a widespread belief among adults in our modern society that the free and easy play times between parents and children are frivolous and nonproductive. The deep conviction that play is trivial is reflected in comments by adults such as "she's only playing," "stop playing around," and "why bother to send him to preschool, all they do is play." Evidence of this attitude is also found in the tendency among parents in recent years to make conscious efforts to teach their children instead of playing with them. Indeed, it is difficult to break loose from the idea that play is a waste of time, particularly in a society that places such a tremendous emphasis on achievement in school, economic success, and the importance of work.

Many parents also believe that children have a natural predisposition toward play. It is expected that children will learn how to play automatically if they are given the right toys, as though playing is "instinctual." Parents tend to assume that it is not necessary for them to participate in play activities because the play needs of children are satisfied by the time spent playing with their peers. The underlying belief is that play is the one thing that children can do for themselves without adult intervention. In fact, our research has confirmed that many parents do *not* play with their children. Parents frequently report that they do not know how to play, or that they do not have time for it. However, studies have shown that while children do engage in a certain amount of spontaneous play, it is not true that children play by instinct. In fact, children have to learn how to play, and unless there is some adult intervention creative play will slowly disappear.

The Importance of Adult-Child Play

Children benefit from adult-child play (as opposed to playing with their peers) in several unique ways. When parents engage in play activities with their children, they can help them solve problems, test out ideas, and explore their imaginations. Play time is an opportunity to encourage the development of a larger vocabulary so that children can communicate their thoughts, feelings, needs, and satisfactions. Play with adults also helps children to interact socially by teaching them how to establish eye contact, to take turns, to compete, and to be sensitive to the feelings of others. Moreover, play is a time when parents can actively respond to children in ways that contribute to their feelings of self-worth and competence. In fact, studies have shown that children tend to be more creative and have fewer behavior problems if their parents engage in make-believe play with them when they are young. For these reasons, adult-child play makes an important contribution to the development of the child. It is an opportunity for children to learn who they are, what they can do, and how to relate to the world around them.

Many parents do not play with their children even if they think it is important and have the time for it. The reason for this is that adults often do not know *how* to play with children. With the exception of play therapists, very few adults are taught this skill. When we analyze the videotapes of parents and teachers who attempt to play with children we find a number of difficulties:

1. Some adults seem reluctant or embarrassed to engage in imaginary play, to crawl on the floor making train noises, or to act out fairy tales. Fathers often report that they feel uncomfortable playing dolls or dress-up games with their sons or daughters. Other parents tell us that they consider imaginary play to be a sign of emotional disturbance.

2. Many adults who do play with children try to structure or supervise their child's play and give the child lessons on what to do: for example, how to build the castle the "right" way. These adults think that they must *teach* their children what to do during play activities. This approach to adult-child play may be due in part to the current attitude among parents that play is frivolous and nonproductive; by imposing structure on play time, parents are attempting to make play a worthwhile activity. The play behavior of these adults is characterized by a lot of commands, criticisms, and corrections. Adults who assume the role of "teacher" also have a tendency to ask a chain of questions such as, "What animal is that?" "How many spots does he have?", and "What shape is that?" In many cases, these questions are not accompanied by answers, feedback, or reinforcement. In addition, adults often place undue emphasis on the "product" of play and attempt to get their children to make a perfect valentine, or complete the puzzle correctly. This style of interacting during adult-child play can make the experience unrewarding for the child and the adult.

3. Some adults unwittingly set up a competitive relationship with their child. When playing board games, for example, they feel that it is necessary to teach their children how to lose gracefully, or that they must play only by certain rules.

4. Sometimes adults become so involved in their own play that they ignore their child altogether and completely take over the child's play. The child is frequently left watching while the parent or teacher plays.

In all of these approaches to play, *the adult has control* over what goes on, and the child is powerless. The situation becomes problematic because the adults tend to *pressure* the children to perform for them. Children react to this in several ways. Some children become wary of trying out new ideas for fear they will make a mistake; thus their creative ideas are stifled. Some withdraw and avoid playing with adults altogether. Others become more dependent on adults to solve problems for them. In general, the children look helpless, unhappy, and show signs of low self-esteem and self-confidence during their play times.

How to Play Effectively with Children

1. Follow the child's leads, ideas, and imagination rather than imposing your own ideas or values. Do not structure or organize play activities for the child by giving commands or instructions. Do not try to teach anything. Instead, imitate the child's actions and do what the child asks you to do.

2. Pace the play at the child's level, allowing plenty of time for the child to exercise his imagination. Do not push the child on to some new activity too quickly because you are bored. Wait until the child decides to do something different. Remember, children's ideas progress much more slowly than adults' ideas.

3. Praise and encourage the child's ideas, creativity, and imagination. Do not judge, correct, or contradict the play. Needless rules and corrections will eventually make a child wary of exploring and experimenting. Remember, it's the "doing" and experimenting that is the most important aspect, not the finished product. Children's play does not have to make sense to adults.

4. Describe enthusiastically what the child is doing and provide supportive comments rather than asking questions or focusing on what the child is not doing. This approach will actively facilitate the child's language development.

5. Role play with the child and encourage make-believe play. Allow boxes and blocks to become houses and palaces, and doll figures to turn into mothers, children, or favorite cartoon characters. Fantasy play allows children to think symbolically and gives them a better idea of what is real and what is not. Role play helps children to experience the feelings of another individual; this helps them understand and be sensitive to the emotions of other people.

6. Be an "appreciative audience" that is attentive to the child's play. Avoid getting involved in your own play and ignoring the child's play. Avoid excessive competition and rules. Losing experiences carry too much weight in the early years and can be overwhelming for young children.

In conclusion, it is important for adults to value play and take part in play activities with children. In addition, adults must learn to play in ways that foster children's self-concept, as well as their social, emotional, and cognitive development. By following the guidelines for effective play presented earlier, you will provide a supportive play atmosphere that allows children to try out their imaginations, explore the impossible and the absurd, test new ideas, make mistakes, solve problems, and gradually gain self-confidence in their own thoughts and ideas. An atmosphere of support and approval gives children an opportunity to communicate their hopes as well as their frustrations. Children live in a world where they have very little power and few legitimate ways to express their feelings. Good play with adults can give children the chance to reduce their feelings of anger, fear, and inadequacy and provides experiences which enhance their feelings of control, enjoyment, and success. A flexible approach to play takes a lot of pressure off adult interactions with children and allows each child to develop into a unique individual who is creative and self-confident.

Other Materials of Interest by the Author

Webster-Stratton, C. *How to Play with Children, Part I* and *Helping Children Learn, Part II.* These two 36-minute videotape instructional programs with accompanying leader's and parent's manuals may be obtained by writing to the author, 1411 8th Ave. W., Seattle, WA 98119.

Recommended Readings

Bruner, Jerome S., Jolly, A. and Sylva, K. (Eds.). *Play: Its Role in Development and Evolution.* New York: Penguin, 1976.

Fein, Greta G. "Play Revisited." In Michael E. Lamb (Ed.), *Social and Personality Development.* New York: Holt, Rinehart & Winston, 1978.

Fein, Greta G. "Pretend Play in Children: An Integrative Review." *Child Development,* 1981, *52,* 1095-1118.

Field, Tiffany, De Stefano, L. and Koewler, J.H. "Fantasy Play of Toddlers and Preschoolers." *Developmental Psychology,* 1982, *18*(4), 503-508.

Garvey, Catherine. *Play.* Cambridge, Mass.: Harvard University Press, 1977.

Jannotti, Ronald J. "Effect of Role-Taking Experiences on Role Taking, Empathy, Altruism and Aggression." *Developmental Psychology,* 1978, *14,* 119-124.

Rubin, Kenneth H. "Fantasy Play: Its Role in the Development of Social Skills and Social Cognition." In Kenneth H. Rubin (Ed.), *Children's Play.* San Francisco: Jossey-Bass, 1980.

Sutton-Smith, Brian. *Play and Learning.* New York: Gardner, 1979.

Properties of Play Toys

Toys are an important part of fostering good play in children; however, it is not always necessary to buy expensive, commercially approved, or "educational" toys. Children are marvelously inventive and, if their imaginations are not squelched by an overly restrictive atmosphere, they can turn almost any object into an interesting play thing.

Basically, good play material and equipment should be:

1. **Safe,** without sharp edges or lead-based paint.

2. **Unstructured** and as free of detail as possible. Unstructured toys such as blocks, play dough, and paints require more imaginary play from children.

3. **Responsive** and versatile. Toys should stimulate children to do things for themselves. Equipment that makes the child a spectator, such as the mechanical duck which waddles and quacks after being wound up, may entertain for a moment but has no play value. The more things a toy does, the less the child does. If the toy renders the child passive it is undesirable.

4. **Large** and easily manipulated. Toys that are too small can be a great source of frustration for young children because the child's muscular coordination is not yet developed enough to handle the smaller forms and shapes.

5. **Pleasurable to touch,** durable and simple in construction. For example, maple hardwood is warm and pleasant to touch as well as durable.

6. **Something that encourages cooperative play.** Housekeeping equipment such as a broom and a dustpan encourages interactions with other children as well as sharing and cooperation.

7. **Within the child's level of skill** and fit in with the child's personality and present interests. However, also take into account your own likes and dislikes so that you will enjoy sharing the toys with your child.

Physical Play

Through play a child acquires and further develops a variety of skills. The first and most obvious skills are physical. Play offers all kinds of opportunities for crawling, walking, stretching, lifting, carrying, reaching, placing, and balancing. This type of play contributes to the child's health and large muscle development as well as the child's small-muscle control and eye-hand coordination.

	Infant/Toddler	Preschooler
Blocks	Milk cartons can be covered with contact paper	Wood blocks
Transportation Toys	Trucks, cars, boats, wagons	Tricycles, scooters
Outdoor Toys	Sandbox (using corn meal instead of sand) with accessory toys for pouring and filling, a swing, a small slide, or a pan of water with a cup	Jungle gyms, wading pools, swings, kiddy cars
Other	Rattles, bath toys, cradle gyms, all sizes of soft balls, pounding toys, walkers/ride-on toys, push and pull toys	

Manipulative and Exploratory Play

This type of play involves problem-solving, manipulating, exploring, and getting control over the activity. It also aids in the development of perceptual motor skills. Even the simplest of toys permits the child to explore the dimensions of space, to manipulate, combine, and reassemble shapes to create new forms, and to become sensitive to the color and texture of materials. Perhaps most importantly, the child learns that he or she can control the process and outcome of the entire activity.

	Infant/Toddler	Preschooler
Sorting and Matching Games	A coffee can with two holes—a round hole for clothespins and a slot for lids	Jigsaw puzzles or wooden inset shape sorters
Construction Toys	Graduated boxes, cups, interlocking blocks, stacking toys (nesting toys), any empty boxes	Legos, log cabins, bristle blocks, models
Art Activities	Yarn, crayons, paint, paper, pipe cleaners, shaving cream or jello	Scissors, clay, play dough, finger paint with chocolate pudding, Etch-A-Sketch
Other	Books, mobiles, bath toys, cradle gyms, squeak toys, mirrors, busy boards, suction toys, saucepans, spoons, any safe kitchen items	Cloth with zippers, buttons and button holes, shoes and laces, zippers and snaps

Symbolic Play*

This type of play involves manipulation of symbols and ideas rather than people or objects. What we mean by this is that in make-believe play children manipulate representations of things rather than the things themselves. Pretend play may appear in children as *early as 18 months* and is found in most healthy children by age three. Imaginary companions often are created by the fourth year of life. Fantasy play steadily increases into middle childhood and then begins to disappear.

Suggestions:

> Puppets—brown bag or hand puppets
> Dress-up clothes box
> Housekeeping toys—dolls, teddy bears, dollbeds, buggies, pillows, tables, chairs, dishes, stools, pots and pans, brooms
> Mud, sand, and water play—for pies, cakes and tea parties
> Pretend telephones, play money
> Pretend play—stores, houses, trains, hospitals, horses
> Books—stories about everyday happenings, special events, calamities and accomplishments

*These play materials can be used with infants one year of age and older.

Games

When play is governed by rules or conventions, it is called a game. Toddlers and preschool children do not really understand board and card games. They may attempt to play a board game side by side but do not interact in a game-like fashion with a clearly defined understanding of the rules of games. It is not until the child is seven to eight years old that he or she will show signs of cooperative interaction and even then the child's understanding of the rules may be somewhat vague. Nonetheless, children can enjoy "playing at" a game with an adult as long as excessive competition and rules are avoided.

Infant/Toddler	Preschooler
Games that require matching, patterning, grouping: find the laundry items that match, colored paint chips or lids, shapes	Dominoes, board games, peg boards, "go fish"
Peekaboo, hide a toy under a blanket for the child to find	Hide-and-seek, tag, catch, follow-the-leader

Stories/Books

If books are introduced to children at an early age, it encourages them to develop a lifelong love of books. Books help infants learn the sounds and meaning of language. Sharing books with toddlers encourages quiet, sustained play, creates parent-child intimacy, and develops language skills. A love of reading lets children explore feelings, fantasies, and the world around them.

Infant/Toddler	Preschooler
Plastic books made from zip-lock bags or plastic holders sewn together. Put different pictures in the "book" each week	Paper books with bright pictures
Books with cardboard pages for turning, biting, and chewing	Blank books for children to make up stories with pictures, art materials, and scribbles
Books with one bright picture per page, a simple story, and not too many words	Nursery rhymes, animal stories, books about everyday happenings
Touch-me books	

Hearing, Speech, and Language Development

JOANNA KISHPAUGH, M.S., SP.-C.C.C

Sacred Heart General Hospital—Home Health Division
Eugene, Oregon

Introduction

During the first three years of development, changes take place almost daily in the way your child uses and responds to speech and language. Many of these changes are so small that they go unnoticed by parents. Often only the most obvious milestones in language development, such as the baby's first words and phrases, receive "bursts" of attention and praise from adults. I know this from personal experience because I became a speech/language pathologist after my son had already passed through the early-language period. In retrospect, I have often wished that I had been more aware of the various subtle stages of speech and language development so that I could have been more actively involved in the process of language acquisition as it occurred. The purpose of this article is to describe the developmental stages so that you can be a more effective "language teacher" and better understand what is happening in your baby's world. Activities to stimulate

162

speech and language skills will be described that you can include in the everyday interactions that you have with your child. Working on speech and language skills with your child is a rewarding, educational, and fun experience for both you and your baby.

An Overview of Speech/Language Development

Before infants can respond to the speech and language portion of their world they must first learn to discriminate one sound from another and to associate meaning with these sounds. Your baby's response to sound begins very early in life. In fact, research has shown that a fetus can respond to sound as early as five months *en utero,* and it is clear that immediately upon birth your baby actively responds to sounds. Many changes and refinements must take place, however, before your baby develops normal perception and hearing discrimination.

Children pass through specific stages of hearing discrimination. The rate and sequence of development are relatively unique for individual children. Each stage described here should be viewed as an approximation of the way in which one set of skills leads to the next. Unless your child deviates substantially from the following guidelines, there is no reason to seek professional advice.

Birth to 4 months. Eye-blinking, eye-widening, or a startle reflex should occur when a baby is in a relatively quiet environment and is exposed to a sudden noise. Infants may also be aroused from sleep by noise. By three to four months babies will usually begin to turn their heads toward the source of a sound.

4 to 6 months. At four months infants will consistently turn their heads to locate a sound. The response is slow and awkward at first, but by six months they will quickly turn their heads to find the source of a sound.

7 to 9 months. By seven months babies begin to locate sounds in a downward plane. At this age babies use a two-step approach: first they look to the side and then down. At nine months babies usually begin to look upward.

9 to 16 months. A two-step head turn is now used to locate sounds coming from above: first the infant looks to the side and then upward.

16 to 24 months. At this age babies can locate sounds by turning directly to either side, up, or down.

Becoming familiar with the various stages of hearing discrimination should help you to "tune in" to your child's hearing response. Try shaking a rattle in these different planes and notice your child's reaction. How did your child move in order to locate the sound?

Mothers generally begin talking to their babies from the moment they first hold them. The mother's voice and gentle intonation are comforting to her baby even though, for the infant, the words have no specific meaning. During the first several years of development your child will spend literally thousands of hours listening to the inflection in your voice and the words that you use. As the primary caretaker, you are the most important speech/language teacher that your child will ever have.

Learning to associate meaning with sounds is the next step in speech and language development. For the first several months after birth, babies spend a lot of time attending to the visual and auditory stimuli in their immediate environment. As a result of this listening, your infant will gradually learn to distinguish your voice from all other voices. This learning takes place when infants are repeatedly exposed to the sounds of their parents' voices in association with meaningful experiences such as being held, comforted, and fed. Over time, and after many trials, the infant learns that a certain voice is connected with being fed, that another voice may be connected with being held in a slightly different way, and so on. As your baby continues to develop, he or she will learn to make increasingly refined associations with sounds. For instance, when the mother says, "No! Don't touch!" the baby learns to recognize that the urgency and intonation in her voice has a *special* meaning. The baby also begins to understand the underlying meaning of the word "no." This process of refinement continues at different rates and levels for a number of years. Your child hears complex adult language, adapts it so that it is compatible with the developmental stage that he or she is in, and eventually incorporates meaning into his or her own language structure.

Skills learned in your baby's first year help lay the foundation for later speech development. During this formative period your baby listens attentively to what you say and learns to discriminate sounds and associate meaning with them. This "listening" behavior is referred to as "receptive" language. It is the language your child hears and learns to understand. "Expressive" language is the ability to communicate needs, ideas, and feelings through gestures, sounds, and talking. Anyone who has traveled to a foreign country has experienced the difference between receptive and expressive language. When trying to master a new language it becomes immediately clear that your ability to understand what people are saying far exceeds your ability to speak the language. Similarly, infants acquire receptive language skills before they learn to express themselves verbally.

Infants typically experiment with a variety of sounds before they begin to produce words. This kind of verbal play is called "cooing" because the most frequently occurring sounds, /k/ and /g/, are produced in the child's throat (for example, "coo" and "goo"). When babies "coo" they are discovering that they can make sounds. If you pay attention to when your baby "coos" you'll notice that it is usually an expression of pleasure. This behavior often occurs when the baby is sitting in an infant seat or has just awakened from a nap. Babies are generally quite entertained by cooing and this behavior is usually their first attempt at solitary play. Somewhere around six to eight months of age, cooing shifts to what is known as "babbling" (cooing behavior typically stops and the /k/ and /g/ sounds disappear and don't reappear until a much later time). Babbling sounds are produced in the front of the mouth and primarily involve the lips (for example, bababa, papapa, mamama). Babbling is a type of sound play that babies use to refine and practice the sounds they will need to make real words.

At 10 to 12 months your child will begin to communicate certain needs to you by using gestures such as reaching or pointing. Speech sounds may or may not accompany these gestures. Generally babies are very interested in listening to speech at this age. You may also notice that your child is getting better at imitating simple phrases such as "bye-bye."

At 12 to 18 months babies usually begin to produce one-word utterances. In addition to practicing sounds, they will attempt to name things. For example, they will say "ba," "mama," "no," "go," etc. Initially "words" will be used in a very general way. "Ba" may mean bottle, ball, blanket, and book. As time goes on, "ba" will gradually be used to refer to one specific object such as ball. By 18 months infants usually have a vocabulary of about 20 to 50 words. As this vocabulary increases, you will begin to notice the emergence of two-word "sentences." A word of caution: the sentences produced by your child won't sound like your sentences, so don't worry if the sounds and words aren't perfect. Your child is simply adapting language to an easier level of speech production.

The period from 18 to 24 months is marked by very rapid growth in expressive language. By now babies are interested in learning the names of things and enjoy talking and communicating. Babbling drops off as more and more new sounds are mastered. By now, an unfamiliar adult can usually understand your child's speech even though he may still use words

166

like "goggie" for doggie or "titty tat" for kitty cat. At about two-and-a-half years of age, children have an expressive vocabulary of approximately 200 to 300 words. They will begin asking questions (e.g., "Where daddy?, "What dat?") and will understand *most* of what you say to them.

At about three years of age your child will have a receptive vocabulary of 800 to 900 words. By this time children can usually follow two-stage commands (for example, "Go get your coat and bring it to Mommy") and may begin using three-word sentences (for example, "Daddy go bye-bye"). Children enjoy talking to themselves all the time now—when they are playing, looking at books, getting dressed, and so on. In fact, it may seem as though your child talks incessantly. This is a good observation because at this age children are almost *exclusively* preoccupied with language learning.

At three to four years, your child may begin to use adult grammar forms such as the "-ing" form of verbs, the past tense of verbs, plurals, etc. Children begin to understand and express location (e.g., in, on) and more than one (e.g., some, two, more). They also start to ask "what," "where," "how," and "why" questions. You may notice that your child now uses language to boss and criticize others. At this age children are capable of carrying on long conversations and their speech is understandable 90% to 100% of the time. By now most of the following sounds will have been acquired: m,n,b,p,t,d,k, g,w,h, as well as all of the vowels. However, children may continue to have trouble producing r,l,s,z,sh,j,ch,f, and v. Don't be alarmed, because these sounds are more difficult and are usually developed much later (in fact, some children still have difficulty with these sounds at six or seven years of age and may require professional help to master them).

Common Problems Associated with Language Development

Hearing Problems

Chronic earaches can be very painful for children and may also result in an intermittent hearing loss. If hearing problems occur frequently or are severe enough, they can reduce your child's ability to discriminate sounds and impede speech and language development. The general information that follows has been included to help parents identify and understand potential problems.

The most frequent cause of ear infections in young children is the common cold. These ear infections occur in an area just behind the eardrum called the "middle ear." Your doctor may use the term "otitis media" (which literally means "middle ear infection") to describe this condition. Under normal circumstances the eustachian tube functions to equalize the air pressure in the middle ear. This tube begins at the middle ear and ends in the throat. When your child has a cold, the eustachian tube may become blocked and no longer aerate the middle ear chamber. Negative pressure then builds behind the eardrum and causes it to be pulled in. As this pressure builds, it draws fluid from surrounding areas that accumulates in the middle ear. If the pressure and fluid aren't reduced, the eardrum will eventually burst and hearing ability may be affected by the scar tissue which develops as the tear heals. If your child complains about a painful earache or you notice that he cries and rubs or pulls at his ear, a trip to the pediatrician is definitely recommended. Medications may be prescribed to alleviate the pain and cure the infection.

To illustrate the impact otitis media can have on hearing, imagine how things sound when you're under water in a swimming pool. This is how some children hear during a middle ear infection—the sounds are garbled and unclear. Obvi-

168

ously this kind of interference can be a handicap during the early stages of language development. This is particularly true if the problem becomes chronic. Some children have otitis media so often that their pediatricians recommend placing Pressure Equalizing (P.E.) tubes in their ears. P.E. tubes are tiny plastic tubes that are surgically inserted through the eardrum to ventilate the middle ear. After the operation, air can pass freely in and out of the middle ear so that negative pressure and fluid cannot accumulate. P.E. tubes sometimes fall out spontaneously as the structures inside the ear grow larger. If this does not happen, the P.E. tubes are removed surgically when the child is four or five years old, depending on the number of ear infections that the child experiences. These tubes are extremely effective and have allowed many at-risk children to hear normally during the early developmental stages that are so crucial to normal speech and language acquisition.

Fluency

Many parents become alarmed when their three-year-old begins to hesitate and/or repeat words or parts of words. This is a normal occurrence at this age because the child doesn't always have control of his or her speech/language system. The repeating, pausing, backing up, holding onto sounds, as well as general confusion in "thinking and talking" are all very normal for young children. They may not know how to put enough words together to express themselves efficiently. Here are some tips for parents who may have concerns regarding what speech/language pathologists refer to as "nonfluent speech."

1. Listen to *what* your child says, not *how* it is said.

2. Be patient while your child is speaking. Don't interrupt or make children start over when they make a mistake. Don't tell children to relax and/or take a deep breath.

3. Don't force your child to talk to others. Resist the

temptation to put children "on show" to entertain grandparents or friends.

4. Don't allow others to laugh or make fun of your child's speech.

5. Remember to provide a model of slow, clear speech.

6. If you are alarmed by certain aspects of your child's nonfluent speech, seek advice from a speech/language pathologist in your area. If you don't know where to look for one, consult a nearby elementary school or university, or look in the telephone directory for a speech and hearing clinic in your area.

Facilitating Language Development

Most children develop normal speech and language abilities with apparent ease and no special help, but others may need some help in acquiring these skills. In either case, there are many things that parents can do to stimulate their children's speech/language skills. Fortunately, most parents do many of these things instinctively. In fact, researchers in child language development have noticed an interesting phenomenon called "mothereze." Mothereze is a style of communication that caretakers use when they talk to babies and young children. It consists of using short, repetitive sentences in a slow, clear manner. It sounds like this: "Ice cream, Johnny. Ice cream. Is it good? Um-umm. It's good, huh? Do you like strawberry ice cream?" You may not be aware of it, but you probably already talk to your child in this manner. "Mothereze" is a natural and easy way to model good language behavior for your child.

In talking to your child it is very important to remember that communication between a parent and child should be pleasurable to both parties. Use your own good instincts. Tune in to what your child can and cannot do. Don't overwhelm your child with demands for speech/language skills that are not within his or her capabilities. The following sug-

170

gestions are examples of things you may already do with your child to stimulate speech/language abilities.

1. Talk to your child. Talk about things going on in your child's environment. You can do this in a "self-talk" style. That is, while you prepare dinner, place the baby near you and label the food and/or utensils that you are using. Say things as naturally as possible. "Mommy is peeling the potatoes. Now I'm cutting the potatoes. Here they go—into the pot. . .one, two, three." Children attend to all kinds of verbal stimulation, so capitalize on this and use everyday situations to "teach" your child about language. When you go shopping, name and label items for your child. Play sound games and word games whenever possible. Keep it fun by maintaining a relaxed and fun atmosphere.

2. Add to what your child says. When your child says something to you, provide more information by offering a well-formed sentence that's slightly longer and adds more descriptive information. For example, when your child says, "Daddy bye-bye," you might respond by saying, "Yes, Daddy's gone to work. He'll be back at dinner time."

3. Read to your child as often as possible. Set aside a certain time each day to sit down and read to your child. Make sure you won't be interrupted. A few minutes just before nap time or bed time is usually the best. As you read to your child "discuss" the pictures in the books. Have your child talk about the pictures if possible, but avoid being overly demanding. Comment on the story yourself and ask questions which encourage participation: "Is the boy sad? That's right, he isn't sad because he's smiling! He must be happy then, right?" or "I wonder why he did that? What do you think? How would you feel? Would that make you sad or happy?" Be dramatic when you read. Emphasize and talk about new words and what they mean. Occasionally ask your child to retell the story (if he is willing) or use the pictures in the book to create a new story.

4. **Provide your child with new experiences by making things with him and allowing him to "help."** Children love to play in water, so allow them to help out by washing the fruits and vegetables or doing the dishes with you. Older children can participate in all kinds of household tasks. An added bonus is that being "Mommy's helper" makes them feel important and gives them a sense of contributing to the family's business. Use these activities as a means of engaging in "conversations" that are pleasurable to both you and your child.

5. **Sorting or classification tasks teach basic concepts.** It is important for your child's speech/language development to learn certain basic concepts such as size, color, shape, same, different, parts of objects, things that go together, etc. You can facilitate your child's knowledge of these important preschool skills by sorting toys, blocks, kitchen utensils and materials, foods, buttons, and other objects. When you do this, talk about the same color, same size, different shapes, and so on. Another way to classify things is to go through old magazines and catalogs with your child. Cut out pictures and paste them into a scrapbook. Group different kinds of cars on one page, toys on another, and so forth. Label the pictures for your child and talk about the similarities and differences in the pictures. Most children love having their own personalized book and will talk about it over and over to anyone who will listen.

6. **Television watching can also facilitate language growth.** Your child will probably want to watch T.V. so make it a positive experience by monitoring what he watches. Shows such as Sesame Street and Mr. Rogers are produced specifically for young children. Try to sit down occasionally and watch these shows with your child and talk about what's going on.

7. **Sing songs and play sound games with your child.** The traditional nursery rhymes, poems, and children's songs are still around for a reason: they are fun and they teach children

sounds, words, and melodies that eventually facilitate speech/language production.

8. Make sure that speech and language are enjoyable activities. Praise and reinforce your child's attempts at speech. You can do this nonverbally by smiling, nodding your head, or hugging; or verbally by saying things like, "I like how you told me about that." Show your child that you understand what he or she has said by getting things that are asked for (within reason) or by paraphrasing what has been said: "Water? You want a cup of water? O.K."

Conclusion

The development and use of speech and language skills is something that is unique to humankind. As adults we rely on these skills to communicate our thoughts, feelings, ideas and desires to others. As parents we teach our children how to communicate these same things, and in the process, we encourage their speech and language development. Hopefully, by understanding the stages of speech and language development, you will be able to appreciate and actively participate in the amazing process by which your child acquires verbal skills.

References

Bloom, Lois and Lahey, Margaret. *Language Development and Language Disorders*. New York: John Wiley & Sons, 1978.

Bush, Catherine. *Language Remediation and Expansion: Workshops for Parents and Teachers*. Tucson, Ariz.: Communication Skill Builders, Inc., 1981.

Northern, J.L. and Downs, M.P. *Hearing in Children*. 2nd ed. Baltimore, Md.: Williams & Wilkins, 1978.

de Villiers, Jill G. and de Villiers, Peter A. *Language Acquisition*. Cambridge, Mass.: Harvard University Press, 1978.

Recommended Readings

Ausberger, Carolyn, Martin, M.J., and Creighton, J. *Learning to Talk Is Child's Play*. Tucson, Ariz.: Communication Skill Builders, Inc., 1982.

Bush, Catherine. *School and Home Program*. Tucson, Ariz.: Communication Skill Builders, Inc., 1980.

Developmental Language and Speech Center. *Teach Your Child to Talk*. Grand Rapids, Mich.: CEBCO Standard Pub., 1975.

Muma, John R. *Language Primer for the Clinical Fields*. Lubbock, Texas: Natural Child Publishing Co., 1980.

For pamphlets about speech/language/hearing development (for example, "How Does Your Child Hear and Talk?"), write to the National Association for Hearing and Speech Action, 10801 Rockville Pike, Rockville, Maryland 20852, or call 1-800-638-TALK.

MEETING 5

Changes in the Lives of New Parents

Goals

To describe the changes that take place in the lives of new parents when they have a baby. The primary focus of the discussion is on stressful changes, although we also want to consider the many positive ways in which the couple is changed by the baby. The general approach will be to identify areas of stress and then suggest some ways to prevent or reduce their impact on the couple's relationship.

Preliminaries. *Share everyone's news.*

Discussion

The Positive Aspects

Ask each group member to describe some of the positive changes that have taken place in her relationship with her partner since the baby was born. In general, so much is said and written about the demanding aspects of being a parent that the rewards hardly get much mention. In a group like this it may seem natural at times to focus on problems because one of our goals is to help provide solutions. In life it tends to be hard to remember the good times during a bad spell, just like it is hard to remember how it feels to be healthy when you are sick. It may help to make a mental checklist of good things to remember to provide some balance when things aren't going so well.

Having a baby can bring a couple closer together. The baby's birth can be a shared experience of lasting richness for the parents, a time of almost unparalleled closeness and rapport. Seeing the baby for the first time is an extraordinary and unforgettable moment. As the baby grows, parents exult and delight in everything about their child as no family friend or relative can. The exquisite love you have for your child compels you to think in new ways about the meaning of life, the future (and particularly the kind of future you want for your child), your relationship to your partner and to your own parents. Having a baby creates for a couple an enduring sense of commitment to a common goal. But this attitude can only be maintained when both parents work together and try to understand what the other person is going through.

The Stressful Aspects

After group members have had a chance to talk about the positive aspects of being parents, ask them to describe some of the ways in which having a baby can put stress on a couple's relationship. Ask them what they do to reduce the impact of these changes. In order to be able to savor the pleasures of parenting, couples must be able to reduce the accompanying stress to manageable proportions. For purposes of discussion, eight major areas of stress commonly reported by new parents are listed. A description of each problem is provided along with some suggestions for dealing with it.

178

1. Financial. Babies are very expensive. Moreover, one parent may not be able to work because he or she is home taking care of the baby. The financial burden may force the working parent to put up with an unpleasant job for the sake of supporting the family—the prospect of being unemployed is especially frightening when there is a new baby.

Suggestions. Financial strain is very difficult and there are no easy solutions. At the very least, arrange to borrow baby equipment and clothing from a friend or relative with a slightly older child. In many communities, civic clubs lease car seats to families that are unable to purchase them. Take advantage of second-hand stores that stock baby furniture, clothing, and toys. Your baby certainly won't be bothered by hand-me-downs. Call the county's public health department for information about low-cost social and medical services in the community that can make your life easier until your financial situation improves.

2. Time availability. Attending to a new baby means having less time for yourself and your partner.

Suggestions. Conserving time requires planning. If you let things run their course, they'll run you as well, leaving no special times away from baby care. Locate a good babysitter and schedule regular times out by yourself or with your partner. Perhaps you could have lunch together once a week or take a walk together on the weekend pushing the baby in a stroller. Take turns caring for the baby so that each person has some time alone to pursue his or her interests. If you can arrange special times together, it can help keep you and your partner from feeling like tired roommates.

3. "What am I doing with my life?" One parent may have an exciting career while the other stays home with the baby feeling bored and unchallenged; or, one parent might have a miserable job while the other is happy to be home caring for the baby. Either situation can cause resentment and lead to more serious problems.

179

Suggestions. At the very least, talk about your feelings. When you do, try to understand your partner's situation and think about what you can do to help. Remember that your partner's feelings are real even if you can't understand them or are confident that those feelings will pass. Being told that "things will look better soon" provides some solace, but it can also sound like disinterest.

4. Resentment. If the baby wasn't planned, or if one parent was more enthusiastic about having a child than the other, it may lead to confrontations such as, "If it weren't for you . . ." or "If it weren't for the baby . . . ."

Suggestions. This sort of argument is nonproductive—it only makes both parents angry. You and your partner are in it together now, regardless of the past. You owe it to yourselves and the baby to accept the responsibility of being parents without resentment, second thoughts, and second guessing. If such arguments start, try to end them as quickly as possible or consider seeking professional counseling.

5. Unfulfilled Expectations. There is nothing easy about being a parent—it takes a lot of effort to take care of the baby's needs, and a healthy couple relationship will suffer if either person stops contributing to it.

Suggestions. Keep in mind that there are no "perfect" babies, children, or parents. Try to keep your expectations within realistic limits and don't judge yourself or other family members too harshly. Think of each new interchange as part of the learning process that is helping you become a better parent and a better person.

6. Emotional and Physical Changes During Pregnancy and After Delivery. There are many physical and hormonal changes that take place, not just during pregnancy, but for a long time after delivery as well. These changes can have a dramatic impact on the mother's emotional state.

Suggestions. Try to be aware of the changes in your body and be patient with yourself. Don't underestimate how fa-

180

tigued both parents can be; rest enough so that you have the energy to solve problems. Keep in mind that the changes in your body can make a difference in the way the world looks to you. As hard as it may be, try to imagine how things would seem if you just felt better.

7. Making the Transition from a Couple to a Family. Having a baby forces both parents to view themselves and each other in a different light. You are now both a partner and a parent. This raises questions about your relationship, such as: Have my feelings about my partner changed? Do we accept each other's parenting style? Do conflicts about parenting have an impact on other areas of our relationship?

Suggestions. To control problems, you must deal with them. Acknowledge that some difficulties are inevitable during the transition to parenthood. Try to talk about potential problems in advance and be prepared to deal with them when they arise. Agree on general solutions or compromises so that you do not have to figure out what to do in the same situations over and over again. It is helpful for partners to give signals when they are tired, angry, or upset so that the other person doesn't jump to the wrong conclusions. The importance of effective communication cannot be emphasized too strongly—it is unfair to expect your partner to read your mind.

Sometimes when a baby seems to be causing problems in a couple's relationship, the baby is merely acting as a catalyst that increases the intensity of problems that were already there. If a problem persists, try to get some outside help while there is still good will between you and your partner. Don't wait until matters escalate and "unforgivable" things are said and done.

Remember to verbalize and show your affection for your partner so that your family life consists of more than just problems and problem-solving. Mention it when your partner looks especially attractive. Occasionally, when the baby falls asleep, forget about your chores and do something fun together.

8. Sex. The changes in your body and the day-to-day child-care routines inevitably alter your sex life by creating new problems or perhaps making old ones worse. These may show up as lack of spontaneity (you can't relax because the baby is sleeping in your room or in a neighboring room and you have to keep the door open to hear the baby), apprehension about possible sexual arousal when nursing or the prospect of leaky breasts during intercourse, fatigue and pain during intercourse, and not feeling sexy because your body has not returned to its prepregnancy shape.

Suggestions. Parents tend to think that these problems are unique to their relationship, but they aren't. Both new parents need love, affection, and support. A hug at the right time can mean a lot. Remember that sex is more than intercourse; giving and receiving pleasure can mean a massage or just holding each other. Try to be honest with each other, exercise some creativity, and keep your sense of humor. Don't feel that you owe the baby constant attention or that going out for an evening with your partner will have to wait until the baby sleeps through the night. Having a babysitter who comes one evening each week can help you and your partner to shift gears and leave the house for a walk, a drive, a movie, or to sit in a restaurant and talk.

Summing up the Discussion

If you think of the couple as the source of the family's strength, then you provide security for your children by keeping your relationship strong and healthy. Remember the things you used to enjoy doing together before the baby was born. Generate some new ideas and interests, and indulge yourselves regularly.

Next week we'll talk about socialization and managing behavior.

Suggested Readings for Meeting #5

Jaffe, Sandra S. and Viertel, Jack. *Becoming Parents: Preparing for the Emotional Changes of First-Time Parenthood.* New York: Atheneum Press, 1979.

Rozdilsky, Mary Lou and Banet, Barbara. *What Now? A Handbook for New Parents.* New York: Scribner, 1975.

Keeping Your Relationship Alive After the Baby Comes

WENDY MALTZ, M.S.W.

Private Practice—Licensed Marriage and Family Counselor
Eugene, Oregon

Perhaps there should be a warning printed on birth certificates similar to those on cigarette packages and diet sodas. It could read: "Caution: Having a baby can be hazardous to your relationship." Then new parents could prepare for the impact that having a baby will have on their primary adult relationship.

I remember coming home from one of my first Birth to Three meetings as a new mother with the bad news. I shared my concerns with my husband, Larry: "Guess what, honey? Today I found out that according to some statistics, marital satisfaction plummets with the birth of the first child. It starts to climb slowly when the child is four, but doesn't surpass the pre-baby level until after the *last* child has left home!" Larry looked a bit alarmed. When he regained his composure, he put his arm gently around me and stated enthusiastically, "Well, *we're* gonna beat the statistics!" It was great to hear him say that—his determination and positive attitude were very reassuring.

As time went on, however, our enthusiasm for "beating the statistics" was slowly tempered by the realities of new parenthood. We knew that our relationship was changing and there seemed to be nothing we could do about it. When we decided to have our second child, our approach was much more realistic. We sat down one night and asked each other in a straightforward way if we were willing to give up the fragments of free time that we had carved out for ourselves and put our intimate life on hold once more. After some discussion, we agreed. It was very matter-of-fact, as though both parties had agreed to make payments on a new car loan.

After becoming a new parent, you probably experienced changes in your relationship as a couple. Some of the changes are good, others not so good. By becoming aware of how and why the negative changes occur you can prevent or minimize many problems and know how to cope with others if they arise. This article will discuss three factors that contribute to the negative impact on the couple's relationship. These are: 1) changes in role expectations and family dynamics; 2) dealing with new life stresses; and 3) breakdowns in couple togetherness, privacy, and sexual relating. This article will describe each of these factors and give strategies and suggestions for what can be done to build and maintain a strong relationship. The goal is to keep your relationship alive so that *both* parents can fully experience the joy of family life with a new child.

Changes in Role Expectations and Family Dynamics

With the arrival of the first baby, new parents automatically assume the roles of "Mommy" and "Daddy." These roles carry with them expectations for how each person should behave that may conflict with relating to each other as a romantically bonded couple. It can be hard to think of your partner as a lover and a playmate when there is a new baby in your

185

home. Is it okay for a "Mommy" or a "Daddy" to act sexy? However disoriented or fatigued you may feel at the beginning, find some ways to put your "Mommy" and "Daddy" roles aside and hold onto the romance in your relationship. Even though becoming a parent means a dramatic shift in identity, this is not all of who you are.

A new baby changes the interaction between family members. Before the baby's arrival, the couple spends their time relating to each other like this:

male ◄─────► female

After the baby joins the family, interactions between family members take place within a triangle like this:

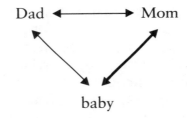

In this new system, one person is always left out—it just isn't possible for three people to interact with each other simultaneously. In most families, because of breastfeeding and/or tradition, Mom is the primary caretaker. As a new bond is formed between Mom and baby, the original bond (and intimacy) between the two adults may suffer. This is usually most evident during the first nine months of the baby's life. New fathers often go through a period of feeling that they have been left out of the flow of things and may become depressed because they have lost the companionship of their female partner. Many fathers feel that the best way to offset this tendency is to become more actively involved in taking care of the baby. Some working fathers make it a point to spend one day each week alone with their baby. Others try to bathe, feed, or change the baby's diapers when they can.

The tendency for the baby to change the interaction between parents can be offset by engaging in activities that allow for more adult-to-adult contact *while the baby is with you.* Taking a car ride (with the baby in the *back* seat) gives Mom and Dad a chance to talk, and gives the baby an opportunity to calm down and take a nap. Putting the baby in a stroller or a backpack for a walk gets the baby out of the house and gives parents a chance to talk, exercise, and be together.

It's easy to forget that the most important bond in the family is the original one between Mom and Dad. The demands of caretaking and concern for the baby may overwhelm and overshadow the important fact that a good relationship between the parents is essential to the well-being of the family— without it, the whole family system is in jeopardy.

Dealing with New Life Stresses

The second way that parenthood can have a negative impact on the couple's relationship is that new babies simply create daily stresses for parents. Some parents talk about raising children as though it is a "trial by fire." Medical emergencies, routine infant care, and lack of sleep gradually take their toll on the coping abilities of the parents. Even "fun" activities such as birthday parties, visits to Grandma's, or trips to the zoo require expenditures of energy that can leave parents feeling drained. If the stress associated with being a new parent is not controlled, it can dramatically reduce marital satisfaction, and impair your own health and your ability to function effectively as a parent.

It is inevitable that there will be periods when stressful events pile on top of each other and the situation becomes critical. Because it is much easier to problem-solve when you are not under stress, it is a good idea if you can develop a "game plan" for dealing with stressful situations *before* they occur. Sit down and try to imagine some of the problems your family might need to cope with. What if one of the parents gets sick? What if *both* parents get sick? What if the babysitter doesn't show? What could you do if one of these situations arises? Have a list of backup babysitters on hand, and make arrangements with friends who are willing to help during illness or emergencies.

Perhaps the best way to prevent or reduce the stress that is experienced by new parents is to learn to work *together* as a team. It's important to focus your energy on supporting each other and remaining friends. Don't allow yourself to view your partner as a problem or the enemy! Stay task-oriented and brainstorm solutions together. Avoid criticizing each other; above all, make *stress* the enemy and figure out ways to deal with it. Don't forget to give each other lots of appreciation for the positive parenting and partnering that is occurring.

A team approach can be used to reduce the stress that comes from providing for the baby's needs. Many couples take turns at child care. They may alternate 20-minute shifts with the baby, allowing the other partner to rest. Decide on who gets the first shift (flip a coin if no one volunteers). Other couples alternate diaper changing so that each person takes a turn doing some of the more demanding tasks.

Couples can also handle times of stress more effectively if they are able to respond to each other constructively. Take time to find out beforehand what your partner needs in order to feel better during times of stress. Also, make sure to share with your partner what you need and respond to. On the next page is a list that can help you identify what each parent needs during stressful periods. Each partner should rate each response with WVM for "want very much," W for "want," and D for "don't want."

During Times of Stress I "Want":   Father   Mother

1. to feel physically close, e.g., sit next
    to you, be hugged   _____ _____

2. to have lots of eye contact   _____ _____

3. to be spoken to in a calm tone of
    voice   _____ _____

4. to be listened to and know that you
    hear what I say   _____ _____

5. to hear suggestions on what I can
    change   _____ _____

6. to brainstorm ideas together for how
    we can resolve the problem   _____ _____

7. to be encouraged to talk   _____ _____

8. to be reassured that you love me   _____ _____

After you have finished, talk about the results. Look for ways to be more responsive to each other during stressful times. This is also a good time to discuss ways to sit and/or touch each other that are conducive to good communication. Some couples find that sitting down and facing each other while they talk helps them communicate more easily; others like to hold hands while they talk. I call this "posturing" and have found that couples who can position themselves comfortably have an easier time problem-solving together. When you talk about how to deal with stress, keep in mind that *both* partners must be willing to make concessions in order to create a cooperative system that works. Expectations concerning what each partner thinks he or she requires at this time *have* to change—individual needs must be put on hold for a while. Good communication requires a lot of give and take, while at the same time preserving mutual and self-respect. If developing communication skills is difficult to learn on your own, seek help from counselors, ministers, books, and classes (some guidelines for effective communication are also provided at the end of this article). Whatever happens, don't allow yourselves to drift apart as a couple.

It's not unusual for each person to want different things. As long as there is a common desire to be responsive to each other, however, these differences can be lived with. Take, for instance, the relatively common situation of the mother who has been home all day alone with the baby while the father has been interacting with lots of people at work. She may have a desperate need for some relief from child care and some adult conversation. But when she asks him about his day, that may be the last thing that he wants to talk about. He may want to relax or be alone for awhile to unwind after coming home from work. A creative solution to this dilemma might be for the mother to take a class in the early evening while the father takes a walk with the baby. Or, the father could relax or exercise for 30 minutes by himself and then take over the child-care duties while the mother relaxes. Later, the couple could get together for some adult time and talk together. Both partners need to be supported by the relationship in order to take some time for themselves. Time spent in self-enhancing activities keeps each person content as an individual, and helps each partner cope with stresses from a "cared for" position. Even when the needs of each parent go in opposite directions, it is possible for the couple to work creatively through the differences so that both parents end up feeling supported.

Many new parents find that dealing with new stresses forces them to structure time as they never did before. Coordinating appointments, child-care responsibilities, individual pursuits, couple activities, and family events can make you feel like an air-traffic controller. And at all times couples must be able to adjust gracefully to the frequent and inevitable

190

changes in plans. The most important activities have to be assigned priorities, and others dropped. To counter persistent tiredness, put sleep high on the list. Socializing, vacationing and sexual relating require a new level of planning to insure that they happen.

To save time and energy, lower your housekeeping standards. The clutter generated by caring for your new baby is frustrating and can become a source of conflict. Now is not the time to strive for an immaculate house, gourmet meals, or a well-trimmed yard. Getting by with the basics is enough of an accomplishment. If there are no clean clothes you can wear what you wore yesterday for one more day, and if you haven't prepared a luscious dinner, you can still find *something* to eat. I remember having hot dogs, canned fruit cocktail, and toast for dinner when our second child was an infant (our four-year-old boy thought it was a great meal!). Get to know the take 'n' bake stores in your neighborhood. Some will even meet you in the parking lot with your dinner if you call ahead of time and tell them you're on your way: "Look for a lady in a dirty yellow car, waving a $5 bill, with a baby in the back seat."

Relax your career and work standards. It's all right to be less aggressive at work; accept a slower pace for achieving goals and advancing in your career. You'll *never* have another chance to experience your child at this early age, but you *will* be able to get back to achieving work-related goals when your child is older. Keep your time commitments at work to a minimum and avoid working overtime if you can.

Breakdowns in Couple Togetherness, Privacy, and Sexual Relating

A good couple relationship needs attention and care to survive. Sometimes you may feel as though the baby is preventing you from being close to your partner. It is inappropriate, however, to place the blame on the baby. Be creative and look for new ways to keep from drifting apart as a couple.

Part of the problem is that you can no longer rely on spontaneous moments to focus on each other. Couples need to nurture their relationships by creating time to check in with each other on a regular basis. One idea is to set aside 10 minutes every day for this. Put the baby down for a rest, then forget about the dishes and the other chores. Make it a priority to focus on each other in a noncritical, loving way. Find out how your partner is *really* doing. Look into each other's eyes; affirm your togetherness. Find new ways to actively strengthen your relationship. Developing the friendship and romantic connection between you nurtures each person. Many new parents make it a policy to go out together at least one night a week. Some hire a babysitter to come one night each week on a regular basis. Others enter into an evening child-care exchange with another couple on a weekly basis. When we had our first baby, Larry and I began meeting for lunch once a week in addition to going out one night each weekend. These times together were very special to both of us because they created the time and space that was necessary for us to focus on ourselves as an intimate pair.

When I give talks to parent support groups, I like to suggest taking an overnight "vacation" together as soon as possible. I must confess, however, that our own first overnighter didn't take place until our first child was two-and-a-half years old and I was pregnant with the second. But I loosened up some and took my next overnighter alone with Larry when our second child was one-and-a-half years old. We got as far as a downtown hotel, but I loved it, and we've been there twice since. Now I'm working on a trip out of town for our next overnighter. Needless to say, most parents are anxious about leaving their babies, but a well-trusted person *can* care for the baby very well and give you both some needed time together.

Most couples experience a dramatic negative change in

their sexual life when the new baby comes. The situation usually improves by the end of the first year. Some of the factors responsible for this include exhaustion, changes in the way the woman views her body, loss of time for spontaneous relating, hormonal changes that reduce the female sex drive, changes in how partners view each other, increased daily stress, and a breakdown in old patterns of sexual courtship. Generally speaking it is the mother who temporarily loses interest in sexual activity.

Most physicians fail to warn couples about the sexual changes that they may experience after childbirth. Instead, most doctors focus on how soon after childbirth sexual relations can be resumed. I recall running into my friend, Molly, at the swimming pool when her baby was three weeks old. She exclaimed, "The doctor said it's okay to have sex—but I'm not telling Jim!" It's not that Molly didn't love Jim, or that she didn't like having sex with him; she was still recovering from having a new baby and was experiencing lots of changes in *her* sexuality as a result. I often joke when I explain to new parents that it's like eating pizza after oral surgery—no matter how much you liked pizza before, it's just not very appealing for awhile. Holding, rocking, feeding, and especially nursing the baby tax the mother's body. Sex may at times be experienced as just another demand. Sex may be more appealing if the mother consistently gets some time to herself to take a bath, read, and otherwise "recharge her batteries."

The challenge for the couple is to go along with this "temporary disability" and not lose the ongoing physical contact with each other that nurtures a healthy relationship. Many couples focus on alternative ways of expressing affection such as hugs, massage, holding hands, and bathing together. In terms of sexual release, this period can inspire the couple to develop new forms of sexual expression that are not limited to intercourse. Many couples find they feel more comfortable with new forms of sexual expression the more they practice them over time. Sexual desire is more likely to be reestablished in an unpressured atmosphere where each partner assumes the primary responsibility for his or her own sexual release and satisfaction. Sex that is nurturing, stress-reducing, and just plain fun will be self-perpetuating.

New parents often encounter some sexually related experiences they may feel unprepared for. Take, for example, being interrupted by a crying baby while having sex or, worse yet, by a little face that pops up from the side of the bed and exclaims, "Hi, Mom! Hi, Dad!" It is not appropriate for children to be present while parents are being overtly sexual. New parents have to learn how to stop their sexual activities at any time and not be too bothered about it. Should you be interrupted, follow up with a hug, a kiss, and a comment, such as, "That was great—hope we can come back to it later." The important thing is to maintain a caring, loving attitude toward each other and not to blame the child.

Children sometimes have a hard time allowing Mom and Dad to be affectionate with each other. They may want to be included in every hug or kiss. I think it's best to include children when they are young and consider hugging as an expression of family togetherness. Parents then need to make sure they get back to being affectionate when they are alone. Children need to learn that parents have a life of their own, a love for each other, and a commitment to their relationship. Although children may express some jealousy, ultimately they like the feeling of security that comes from the affection that Mom and Dad show for each other.

New parents need to feel they have some private space of their own in the home. One way of accomplishing this is for the couple to view their bed as an oasis that is "off limits" to children and stress. Children can be encouraged in a gentle, positive manner to respect the parents' need to sleep alone. "You can come into bed with us for a little while, but then we'll move you back to your own snuggly bed. Mommy and

Daddy miss each other during the day and we like sleeping by ourselves at night. Sleeping in our bed alone together and doing other things together like going out in the evening help us to be happy parents."

The first several years of parenthood challenge us as individuals and as partners to provide for a growing child's needs while also providing for ourselves. The key to good parenting is having the ability to place the child's needs and the family's needs before your own; the key to long-range family happiness is to maintain a strong, healthy bond between the two parents. I recall a parents' support-group meeting that I spoke at in which a woman said that she felt like embroidering a big sign for her home saying, "And this too will pass!" It is easy to forget how fleeting the time with a new baby is when you are feeling overwhelmed. Kids grow up and become more independent. They learn to fix their own meals, play by themselves, and spend time with friends. You will probably look back at these early years and feel that they went by all too quickly. By actively facing the challenges of new parenthood as a team, you can build the foundation for many years of family happiness and keep the relationship between you and your partner alive.

Recommended Readings

Block, Joel D. *The Magic of Lasting Love.* New York: Simon & Schuster, 1982.

Dorman, Marsha and Klein, Diane. *How to Stay Two When Baby Makes Three.* Buffalo, New York: Prometheus Books, 1984.

Jaffe, Sandra S. and Viertel, Jack. *Becoming Parents: Preparing for the Emotional Changes of First-Time Parenthood.* New York: Atheneum Press, 1979.

A Workshop Exercise

Directions

The following is a workshop exercise for couples in Birth to Three. Divide the participants into five groups and have each group choose a scenario from the list below. Discuss the scenarios using the questions provided. After the groups have had enough time for the participants to exchange thoughts, form a larger group to share the ideas that have been generated.

1. **Unplanned and Overwhelming.** It was an unplanned pregnancy. Neither Colin nor his partner, Mary, were sure they were ready to get married, let alone have a child. Mary chose not to terminate the pregnancy, and Colin, feeling some commitment to Mary, decided not to leave. Their baby, Tony, has had more of an impact on their lives than either of them expected. Both Mary and Colin feel trapped by the financial burden and constant demands of baby care. Lately, Colin has started to become angry with Mary with little provocation, and threatens to leave her if she asks him to become more involved in Tony's care. Mary is depressed, overwhelmed, and feels all alone.

2. **Supermom/Working Dad.** Marsha quit work when Josh was born. Her husband, Jim, works full time. Marsha's whole life is now devoted to Josh's care; she prides herself in knowing what he needs and how to handle him. Jim would like to be more involved with Josh but feels that he cannot live up to Marsha's standards. When he takes care of Josh, Marsha often criticizes his style. Jim is ready to give up trying. The tension this situation has produced is putting a strain on their marriage.

3. **Sexual Blues/Emotional Needs.** Steven and Ann had a good sex life together before Megan was born. For Steve, having sex was the way he most directly showed his love for Ann and felt her love for him. Since Megan's birth, Ann has had

little or no interest in sex, claiming she is tired or sore in her genital area. Focusing on sexual thoughts is hard for her. Steven misses the intimate moments with Ann and feels rejected by her. Ann wants Steven to be emotionally supportive of her at this stressful time in her life.

4. Baby Upstages the Marriage. Since Timmy's birth, Fred and Mona have been infatuated with him and their new roles as "Mommy" and "Daddy." The focus of their marriage is caring for Timmy's needs and attending to his development. Fred and Mona let Timmy sleep in their bed with them every night and take him wherever they go. Fred and Mona will not go to a party or restaurant if they can't bring Timmy, and they have juggled their schedules so that no outside child care is ever necessary. But Fred and Mona are not happy and each of them secretly wonders where the relationship between the two of them has gone.

5. Who's Working Harder? Emily devotes her daytime hours to Shannon's care. She changes her, feeds her, rocks her, does errands with her, and occasionally attends a baby-swim class with her. Emily also takes care of all the major housekeeping tasks. She often feels exhausted at the end of the day, complaining that this current routine is harder than any "real" job she ever had. Emily wants her husband, Bill, to help out with household chores and be more involved with Shannon's care. Bill works a long day trying to stay on top of the demands of his job, realizing that at present he is the sole breadwinner. Bill figures that Emily is doing fine with Shannon and he prefers spending his evenings relaxing by himself or attending to work that he has brought home with him.

Discussion Questions

> 1. Describe the situation from the point of view of each partner. What are they feeling? What fears and worries might they be having? What hesitations might they be having about sharing their feelings with each other?

197

2. What might happen if they don't work through the situation?
   3. What do they need to talk about?
   4. What are some creative solutions/options they could try to make the situation better?

Guidelines for Effective Partner Communication

   1. Choose a convenient time and place for both partners to discuss important issues (make sure that it is a time when you are least likely to be interrupted). State what you feel and need clearly. Begin sentences with, "I feel..." (state a feeling), or "I need..." (be specific). Avoid using the word "you" a lot.

   2. Communication is at least 50% nonverbal. Try to make what you say consistent with your facial expression and body language.

   3. Deal with one issue at a time.

   4. Regularly practice active listening skills. Let your partner know that you understand and care about what he or she is feeling and experiencing. This can make an important contribution to the feelings of intimacy between you.

   5. Avoid making assumptions about your partner's reactions or the reasons for your partner's behavior. This often distorts reality and creates distance between partners. Accept and honor your partner's feelings—don't try to talk your partner out of feeling a certain way.

   6. Avoid accusations, blaming, put-downs, criticisms, name calling, or labeling. It's important not to use words like "always" and "never." Judging your partner can result in a defensive reaction and make effective communication difficult.

   7. It takes practice to communicate effectively in a relationship. It is important not to get discouraged if initial attempts seem awkward. Be persistent in expressing your needs, but allow time for your partner to make changes or accept new ideas. Effective communication increases self-esteem and makes partners feel close to each other.

MEETING 6

Socialization and Managing Behavior

Goals

To discuss the role that parents play in the socialization of young children. Socialization is the process by which children learn the rules of society and how to get along with other people. The topic of how parents manage the behavior of their children is interrelated because it is the means by which young children are taught to distinguish what is appropriate from what is not. The discussion will be focused primarily on describing some of the different approaches to managing children's behavior.

Preliminaries. *Share everyone's news.*

Discussion

Socialization

Have the group discuss the meaning of the term "socialization." Ask group members to talk about how they were

201

raised, and how they plan to raise their own children. Socialization is the process by which children learn the rules of
society and how to respond appropriately to the people
around them. Children are gradually socialized by interacting
with people. Initially, the child's parents and siblings are the
primary influence—babies and toddlers learn most of their behavior from other family members. This process often takes
place without much conscious effort on the part of the family
members involved. All that is required is for parents and siblings to spend time interacting with infants. If you are consistent in the way that you respond to your baby's behavior, he
or she will quickly learn how to relate to you and to other
people.

Socialization is not only determined by the way in which
parents interact with their children, but also by the way in
which children learn to respond to their parents' behavior.
Your baby is studying you all the time and can distinguish
your states of mind at quite an early age because you behave
differently toward the baby in different circumstances. When
you are feeling good, you are more likely to be playful; when
you are angry or tired you are more likely to handle the baby
impatiently. Your baby is able to perceive cues about your
mood that you may not think are obvious. This sensitivity to
the mood and feelings of others is very much a part of the socialization process—it is essential for learning how to respond
to others appropriately.

In a broader sense, it is through socialization that children
establish (or adopt) a system of values and beliefs. It is the vehicle for developing a sense of morality and self-esteem. Socialization is a complex learning process that takes place slowly through many small steps. As your child grows older and
comes into contact with other children and adults, these people also contribute to the socialization of your child. It is up to
parents to give their children a head start on learning skills
such as sharing, empathetic listening, and caring for the feel-

ings of others that are necessary for developing satisfying relationships with other people.

Parents must consciously deal with the process of socialization when they consider the issues involved in managing their children's behavior (we have tried to avoid using the term "discipline" in this discussion because of the negative connotations attached to it). There are many different approaches to managing behavior (the annotated reading list provides references to some of them under the heading, "Discipline and Childrearing Primers"). The methods you use will depend upon your social setting, personal philosophy, and confidence in the evidence that particular strategies work. Rather than advocating any one set of rules, we will describe a general approach to thinking about managing behavior. The underlying ideas have been taken primarily from "social learning theory" which assumes that children learn most of their behavior from other people. By looking carefully at the interactions you have with your children, you can see how you are shaping their behavior purposefully as well as inadvertently. Once you understand the impact of your behavior on your child, you can be more consistent in strengthening the behaviors that you like and discouraging those that are inappropriate.

Encouraging Behavior

Ask the group to talk about some ways to encourage behaviors in children. This topic has been divided into six approaches that are commonly used by parents.

1. Talking to your child. Simply talking to your child is one way to encourage certain behaviors. For example, when a parent takes a toddler for a walk, pointing out a flower and helping the child to touch and smell it, this encourages the child to explore the world. Many other desirable behaviors such as independent play and sharing with others are acquired and/or maintained in this way. Simply stating what you like (and don't like) about your child's behavior is sometimes enough to change things for the better.

2. Using attention and praise. Give your child attention when he or she does something that you want to encourage. Don't let the good moments and small achievements go unnoticed if you want them to happen more often. For example, suppose that you have been reading the newspaper while your baby plays quietly nearby. Acknowledge the accomplishment by saying, "What are you doing over there? Are you playing? What a wonderful baby!" and then play with the baby for a few minutes. You are encouraging the child to play independently and also teaching the child that good behavior is one way to receive attention from parents.

Praise, like attention, can be used for encouraging specific skills as well as general behaviors. For example, if you see your baby place one block on top of another for the first time, say something like, "Oh, boy, look at that! That's great! Let's try another one. . . . " The baby is likely to respond by continuing to experiment with the blocks and then will look up, expecting the same positive response.

3. Showing physical affection. All normal babies and children respond positively to physical affection, such as hugs and kisses. When your baby does something wonderful, show your delight physically. This encourages both the specific behavior that you like and strengthens your overall relationship with your baby. Showing affection helps your baby to "bond" to you.

4. Tangible rewards. Parents often reward good behavior with something tangible such as a treat, a toy, or a special privilege. An example of this would be giving your little boy an ice cream cone for being patient at the barber shop. Some parents consider this to be "a bribe" and feel that children should be well behaved without being rewarded for it. However, if you occasionally buy ice cream for your child anyway, it certainly makes sense to do it at those times when your child has done something that you want to encourage.

5. Modeling. Children "learn by example" and look up to you as a model of appropriate behavior, especially in unfamiliar situations. For example, if your baby encounters a dog for the first time at a friend's house, show the baby how to pet it; convey to your child your own enjoyment of animals and respect for them. Many aspects of how your children behave as they mature are taken, or "copied," from you (for example, how they show anger or cope with frustration, how they show love and affection, and how they, in turn, raise their own children). Without attempting to be perfect, try to provide a good model for your children to follow.

6. Shaping. Most behaviors and skills are too complex to learn on the first try. The general idea is that each new skill will at first be only a rough approximation of the fully developed skill or behavior. Remembering this will keep you from having unrealistic expectations and help you to recognize the early signs of an emerging skill. We do this naturally when we teach children to speak because it is such a complicated skill. At first, any utterances are rewarded with attention and praise. Later on, the baby must say "ba" for "ball" to receive the same positive response from his or her parents. Finally, only the correct pronunciation of the word "ball" is worthy of attention. Make sure to reward successive approximations of a new behavior and raise the standards slightly after each successful performance. Setting goals that are too difficult to achieve will frustrate both you and your child.

Discouraging Behaviors

Have the group discuss some ways to discourage unwanted behaviors in children. This topic has also been divided into six approaches that are commonly used by parents.

1. "Natural consequences." One way that children learn what to do and what not to do is to experience the natural consequences of their actions. If, for example, your child argues about putting on gloves, it may be better to let him experience a little of the discomfort of cold hands than to argue about it. This empirical approach of letting your child "try it and see what happens" works in many situations. However, it is clearly not the approach to use when the natural consequences are too dangerous (for example, playing in the street) or when your child is not old enough to understand or remember the connection between cause and effect.

2. Withdrawing attention. When children behave inappropriately, withdrawing attention is sometimes a powerful way to change their behavior. For example, when your child screams at the supermarket because you are unwilling to buy the candy or toy he demands, don't comfort him, reason with him, or let yourself get drawn into his tantrum. He will usually stop crying when he sees that the tantrum doesn't have the desired effect on you. This will probably take some self-control on your part, but it can be effective.

Like many aspects of responding to your child, there are no firm rules that dictate exactly how to do it. If you withdraw your attention too often, your child may feel rejected; not using this technique enough may lead you into frustrating arguments and confrontations with your child. It is up to you to decide what fits your personal philosophy and your relationship with your child. Some parents let their children "cry it out" when they are fussy at bedtime; other parents try to rock their babies to sleep. The decision is up to each parent, but if what you are currently doing does not seem to work, try another approach. Our purpose here is to provide you with a survey of alternatives from which to choose.

3. Giving "I" messages. When a child's behavior upsets you, it is all too easy to make your response sound like, "You are a bad child." It is better to respond by saying, "I don't like it when you leave your toys all over the living room." This is in contrast to giving "you" messages such as, "You're always so messy." The underlying assumption in this approach is that the child respects you and will try to accommodate your needs and wishes if you make them clear without rejecting or humiliating the child.

4. Removal of privileges. Activities like watching television, going to a friend's house, or seeing a movie are privileges that children enjoy. Although children may take these things for granted, their parents need not. If your five-year-old refuses repeatedly to clean up a cluttered bedroom, then try curtailing television privileges for that day. Your child will hardly suffer and may get the point. Don't try this strategy, however, unless you are certain that you can follow through and keep the television off.

5. Physical punishment. Many parents use physical punishments such as spanking and slapping to discourage undesirable behavior. Physical punishment is effective in discouraging behavior—it works immediately, and if the punishment is very severe, it doesn't need to be repeated very often. However, physical punishment also exacts a price. It makes children feel helpless, humiliated, and erodes their self-esteem. It can also make your child feel resentful and create distance between you and your child. This type of punishment is particularly destructive when it is delivered erratically by a moody or angry parent.

If you feel that physical punishment is acceptable, reserve it for extreme behavior and do not use it as the primary means of controlling children. Never punish your children when you feel like you have been pushed beyond your limit. Send them to their room and give yourself some time alone to calm down. Call a friend or step outside for a few minutes. We all have different amounts of tolerance for "impossible" behavior, and on some days we may have less patience in reserve than on others. Try to recognize when you're close to your breaking point and do something to calm yourself down before you get there. Often the problem may have more to do with other factors in your life than with the child.

6. Time out. A nonviolent alternative to physical punishment is to remove the child from the setting in which the behavior problems occur. During time out the child is put in a bathroom or other uninteresting room that has been prepared by removing all hazardous objects. For example, let's say that your five-year-old has been starting fights with his three-year-old brother all afternoon. Suddenly you hear the three-year-old yell, "No, that's mine!" and start crying. As you round the corner, the five-year-old is knocking down the block creation that the three-year-old had very carefully built. You decide to discourage the five-year-old's behavior by putting him in time out. State the problem clearly. "Okay, what's going on here? It's not fair to knock down your brother's blocks. You can either play cooperatively together, or leave each other alone. Now I'm putting you in time out for five minutes." Take the child by the hand and lead him to the bathroom. Set a kitchen timer for five minutes and do not let him out until the bell rings. If at first your child starts kicking the door or yelling, add a minute to the timer. Make sure the child knows that, by saying, "Okay, let's be quiet in there, that's an extra minute!" Note that a child should be put into time out for a number of minutes roughly equivalent to the child's age (for example, five minutes for a five-year-old). If your child refuses to cooperate, use backup punishments such as losing television privileges.

Time out seems to work for several reasons: 1) it interrupts the problem situation; 2) it keeps the child from receiving further attention for misbehaving; 3) it gives both parent and child a chance to "cool down" and think about what is going on; and 4) it is unpleasant enough to feel like a punishment without actually hurting the child.

Some General Considerations
Managing Your Own Feelings and Behavior
Ask group members to talk about the thoughts that run

through their minds when they feel they have absolutely had it. What are some of the ways that they cope with these feelings? All of the strategies for encouraging and discouraging behavior that we have just discussed assume that parents are calm and rational when they are dealing with their children's behavior. The ideal mother never raises her voice or loses her patience, has unlimited energy, and always knows the right thing to do. But this is hardly the case for most of us. Knowing that we have some good strategies at our disposal can help us to maintain our equilibrium. However, we all have bad moments and at those times we may be amazed at the rage that small children can provoke in us. When our sleep deficit is too great or we have run out of strategies to try, the baby that we adore can trigger murderous thoughts. Children also change in fundamental ways as they pass from one developmental stage to the next. The same child for whom you felt intense love as an infant can incite absolute fury as a two-year-old. At times, you may find yourself wondering why you wanted a baby in the first place. What do you think about doing with the baby at these moments? One mother in a Birth to Three group said she wished she could make a hole in the living room window just big enough for the baby so she could fling him through it! It can be fascinating and a real relief to hear everyone's accounts of their worst moments and share coping strategies.

These feelings are relatively common among parents. To keep them under control it helps to remember that much of what seems irritating about your two-year-old's behavior is part of a normal and necessary developmental phase (we have all heard of the "terrible two's"). Children need to test their environment, including their parents, in order to grow up. The docile, compliant two-year-old is perhaps more cause for concern than his stubborn, tantrum-prone counterpart. Thinking about your child's developmental age can help you gauge whether he or she can really live up to your expectations. Are you asking for the impossible?

It can also help to try to see the world from the baby's perspective. Some babies just have a more volatile temperament than others. There may be hereditary factors contributing to behavior problems, or biological factors, such as teething or colic, that make the baby irritable. Even though it may have nothing to do with parental handling, the baby's volatility can get everyone in the household into a frenzy.

Even the worst phases pass. Moreover, every new interaction is a chance to start over. Few things the average parent does make an indelible and unforgivable mark on a child. Babies don't hold grudges. If you have been irritable and short-tempered with your child, try to regain your composure and start over.

Of course, preventing troublesome behavior is better than coping with the behavior or responding to it. Sometimes we can anticipate and prevent conflict situations. For example, "baby-proof" the house by removing dangerous or fragile objects that the baby might not treat respectfully. Getting down on your hands and knees may reveal irresistible temptations from your baby's point of view. If your baby insists on pulling all the books out of a low bookshelf, take the easy way out and replace the books with toys for the time being. Another strategy is to distract the baby before things get out of hand. Babies' attention spans are short and a permitted object can usually be substituted for something that you don't want the baby to play with. With slightly older children you can let the child choose from among alternatives you can live with. For example, "Do you want to take the rubber duckie or the sponge into the bath with you?" rather than, "Are you ready to take a bath now?" In that way, you're encouraging exploration and decision making, rather than engaging in the sort of impatient yelling, slapping, ordering about, and frequent "no's" that depress the child's curiosity and lock the parent into a cycle of escalating tension. Babies have to investigate their environment and make choices. It is up to the parents to try to structure things so that the baby has freedom to explore safely without getting into trouble at every move.

Parenting Styles

Each parent has his or her own style of living with children and socializing them. Because of this, you and your partner are bound to relate differently to children. In general, it is best to try to understand and tolerate your partner's approach. At the same time, however, it is important to talk about some of the things that each of you do differently. Try to come to a consensus about major differences such as whether or not slapping and spanking are appropriate punishments. Also try to be sensitive to those times when your partner is feeling pushed to his or her limits, and do something to help out.

Summing Up the Discussion

For most parents, it is hard to see the forest for the trees when caring for an infant. When you are an integral part of the socialization process, it is sometimes difficult to see the small changes that are taking place. But regardless of your own perception, it is true that at the end of each and every day your child is different from who he or she was the day before. This meeting has attempted to describe some of the ways that parents shape their children as they grow. By being more aware of the impact that our actions have on our children's behavior, we can be better parents.

Next week we'll discuss nutrition and starting solids.

The material for this meeting has been adapted from *Active Parenting* by Patterson and Kishpaugh, Castalia Publishing Company, Eugene, Oregon, in press.

211

Suggested Readings for Meeting #6

Briggs, Dorothy Corkille. *Your Child's Self-Esteem.* New York: Doubleday Dolphin, 1975.

Crary, Elizabeth. *Without Spanking or Spoiling: A Practical Approach to Toddler and Preschool Guidance.* Seattle, Wash.: Parenting Press, 1979.

Fraiberg, Selma H. *The Magic Years: Understanding and Handling the Problems of Early Childhood.* New York: Scribners', 1959.

Lerman, Saf. *Parent Awareness.* Minneapolis, Minn.: Winston, 1980.

Patterson, Gerald R. *Living with Children.* Champaign, Ill.: Research Press, rev. ed., 1976.

Helping Your Child Learn Self-Control

BEVERLY I. FAGOT, PH.D., RICHARD HAGAN, PH.D., AND KATE KAVANAGH, PH.D.

Oregon Social Learning Center
Eugene, Oregon

For the last three years, we have been engaged in a study of families with one- and two-year-old children. We are trying to find out more about the relationship between different parenting styles and the child's social development. The purpose of this article is to share some of the findings from our research project with parents who have young children.

Our research indicates that parents start to worry about controlling their child's behavior when the child starts crawling and getting into things. We know that a very young child really doesn't have much ability to control his or her own behavior, but this does not mean that it is too early to start using some types of disciplinary measures. It takes time for children to learn what parents like and don't like about their behavior. After many trial and error experiences in which some behaviors receive a positive response from parents and others do not, very young children learn to discriminate appropriate behaviors from those that are inappropriate. Children gradually develop self-control as they internalize these experiences and learn to keep track of what they are doing so that they can prevent themselves from engaging in inappropriate behaviors (that is, they are able to "discipline themselves"). Rather than thinking about discipline as punishment, it may be more useful to think about it as a way to help your child learn self-control.

Discipline is an important part of your responsibility as a parent. As your child grows older, your role as a parent will change along with your child's behavior. Babies and very young children require almost constant attention. They have so little control over themselves or their environment that the task of managing them is difficult for parents. It is important to design an environment where the baby is as safe as possible, and then identify several critical things that you want to help the child learn (for example, not to draw on the wall with crayons). With time, your child will learn the rules of the household and the rules for getting along with other people (for example, not interrupting while others are talking). This makes the job of child management much easier for parents— the child is developing self-control and the things that you are working on are less critical (for example, your child stops throwing food on the floor but needs better table manners). Try to take a long-range view of things. Although the changes in your child's abilities and behavior are slow at first, he or she is learning all of the time.

Some Points to Remember

1. Teach self-control. The first point to remember about discipline is that you are trying to help the child learn self-control. If you approach the task with the idea of forcing the child to "mind or else," you are setting the stage for years of confrontation. Like every other difficult job, teaching children self-control should be approached with humor and perseverance. You and your child will both make mistakes, but fortunately you have a lot of chances so that one badly handled confrontation does not spell disaster.

2. Understand your child's capabilities. Another important issue in disciplining your child is being sensitive to his or her capabilities. Parents often choose as a point of confrontation a behavior that is really beyond the child's control. For instance, two-year-olds are still very clumsy at small-motor activities so they are not necessarily being naughty when they make a mess of their food at the dinner table. Also, don't read adult motivations into your child's misbehavior. An eighteen-month-old child who hits another child to obtain a toy needs to learn that hitting is inappropriate behavior, but also remember that the child doesn't understand the rights of other children and how they feel; the child is not doing this to hurt the other child, he or she merely wants the toy and knows no other way to get it. Your success in teaching the young child self-control is determined at least in part by how sensitive you are to your child's abilities in terms of motor behavior, social skills, and language comprehension. Make sure that the things that you are working on with your child are within his or her range of skills.

3. Agree about discipline. Everyone who will be sharing childrearing duties should discuss the types of behaviors that are unacceptable and come to an agreement on appropriate behaviors and values for the child. It is important to negotiate differences that arise in discussing these issues. We find that parents who disagree on discipline confuse their children, and that these children have many more problems later on.

4. What to do. Next, you should choose some discipline techniques that are compatible with your approach to parenting. This is often a problem for parents because there are so many perspectives on discipline in books and magazines. The advice that is offered in published sources is often contradictory and confusing for parents to interpret. You may read that

215

children should only receive natural consequences for their acts, but as a parent of a very young child you know this advice cannot always be followed because it can mean exposing your child to something that may cause permanent harm. Or you may read that children should be allowed to explore the world without frustration, but you quickly find out that part of your responsibility as a parent is to stop the child from engaging in certain behaviors, and if that step is not taken, the child quickly becomes an unpopular tyrant. You may believe in some form of the dictum, "spare the rod and spoil the child," but it is dangerous to spank very young children because they are easily injured. Furthermore, there is every indication that spankings are not an effective way to help your child learn self-control. It is easy to see how the many options available and the subtle aspects of "when to" and "when not to" can become very confusing for parents.

5. **Instructional discipline.** Our suggestion is for parents to use something that we call "instructional discipline." To be effective, discipline must stop misbehaviors *and* teach the correct or appropriate behavior. This means that children should be given a chance to recognize that what they are doing is wrong, and then be given a chance to change it. If this doesn't work, then a consistent but mild form of correction should be used.

The disciplinary technique that we recommend using with young children (ages two through 10) is called "time out." This technique is relatively simple and very effective. The child is told that his or her behavior is inappropriate and is given a chance to behave correctly. If the inappropriate behavior continues, then the parent calmly tells the child that he or she is going to time out. The child is then put in a boring place for a few minutes. When the child has finished his or her time out, the incident is over and there is no more discussion of the event.

This method of discipline has several advantages. First,

the child's behavior is clearly labeled as inappropriate so that the child knows what he or she is being corrected for. The child is given a chance to comply, but if this doesn't happen the child is put into a situation that clearly indicates he or she was in the wrong. Next, time out is nonphysical and there is no chance for the confrontation to escalate into a battle. In a recent study, we found that only about 25% of parents thought spanking was a good way to teach children, but spanking was occasionally used as a method of discipline by 80% of the parents surveyed! However, physical encounters do not teach children self-control and they often leave the parents feeling confused and guilty. Finally, time out gives the child and the parent a chance to cool down and start over again. We find in our research and clinical work that the consistent application of this type of discipline gives parents a powerful tool that works with their children, and gives children a chance to understand what is expected of them. Many times we find that children will put themselves in time out, which suggests that they are developing self-control.

6. **When not to discipline.** There are times when you will have to decide whether or not to try to make a very young child behave as you wish. If your child is throwing food in a restaurant and then throws a temper tantrum when he or she is told to stop, what should you do? This is not the place for a discipline encounter, and so your best strategy is to take the child away from the situation until he or she settles down. When you are embarrassed, tired, or upset the best approach is to put the child in a quiet place while you both calm down. It is very hard to be a successful teacher during crises and periods of high stress.

7. **Encourage positive behavior.** Parents often think of teaching self-control in terms of stopping undesirable behavior, but remember that you want the child to know how to behave appropriately in addition to knowing what is inappropriate. When your child does something that you like, let him

or her know how pleased you are. When your child obviously refrains from some forbidden act, compliment him or her. Some parents feel that compliments are bribes and expect their children to be automatically on their best behavior, but for young children this is unrealistic. They need a great deal of feedback on what is right and what is wrong in order to learn how to behave and get along with people. Encouraging positive behavior in children not only leads to increases in those behaviors, it also results in parents spending less time discouraging undesirable behaviors.

Conclusion

We believe that it is possible to teach young children self-control without coercive techniques. Letting children know what is appropriate does not frustrate them; it does not stifle their creativity or lead to future problems. Children who understand the rules of their family are happier and are getting a head start on becoming a caring person.

Recommended Readings

Canter, Lee. *A Parent's Resource Guide*. Washington, D.C.: American Guidance Service, 1984.

Clark, Lynn. *SOS: Help for Parents*. Bowling Green, Kentucky: Parents Press, 1985.

Dorr, Darwin, Zax, M., and Bonner, J.W. *The Psychology of Discipline*. New York: International Universities Press, 1983.

Patterson, Gerald R. *Families: Applications of Social Learning to Family Life*. Champaign, Ill.: Research Press, rev. ed., 1975.

MEETING 7

Starting Infants on Solid Foods

Goals

To reduce the anxiety and uncertainty experienced by parents when babies are ready for the transition to solid foods. The discussion is meant to supplement the basic information that most parents have been given by their physicians. If the group is interested in obtaining more detailed information, consider the idea of inviting a nutritionist to be a guest speaker.

Preliminaries. Share everyone's news.

When to Introduce Solid Foods

Ask the group for suggestions concerning when to introduce infants to solid foods. If your child had been born in this country around the turn of the century, you probably would have been instructed not to offer your baby peas until around his or her third birthday. At the other extreme, in the mid

1950s, many pediatricians were recommending that solid foods should be given to babies who were only a few weeks old. Now, in the 1980s, nutritionists feel that solid foods are important for growth and the development of an appetite for foods other than milk, but four to six months is the suggested age to start.

Waiting until the baby is four to six months old to start on solid foods has several advantages. First, babies can move their tongues and swallow better, which desensitizes the gag reflex. Second, better head control and the ability to sit upright make feeding easier and allow babies to turn their heads to indicate when they are full. This head-turning response helps parents to avoid overfeeding. Third, babies are less likely to develop allergies to certain foods at this age. Fourth, introducing solid foods too early (before the age of four months) can interfere with the way that iron is absorbed from breast milk. Although there is only a moderate amount of iron in breast milk, it is very well absorbed by infants.

First Foods for Babies

Commercially prepared rice cereal for infants is an acceptable first food. It is generally recommended because it is the least allergenic grain, has a simple flavor, and is fortified with iron. You can give the baby cereal at whatever time of the day is convenient, but don't let it interfere with the quantity of milk or formula taken as this is still the baby's primary source of nutrients. Some babies refuse solids when they are very hungry and are too frantic to do anything but drink. Nurse or bottle feed the baby at least a small amount, until he or she is relaxed enough to try again.

Once cereal has been introduced, vegetables or fruits can be added to the baby's diet. A new food can be tried about every five days. Watch for signs of an allergic reaction such as a rash, runny nose, gas, cramps, vomiting, diarrhea, coughing, or irritability (these symptoms will usually appear within five

222

days). The foods that most commonly produce allergic reactions in babies are wheat, uncooked cow's milk, citrus, chocolate, corn, egg white, cinnamon, and pork. Many of these foods can easily be avoided until the baby is between nine and 12 months old, although some parents introduce them earlier and their babies have no apparent problems. If there is a family history of allergies, it is sensible to be more cautious.

Honey in any form, even pasteurized, is a food to avoid completely during the baby's first year. It can be contaminated with spores of the bacteria that cause botulism. These spores cannot grow in the intestines of older children and adults, but are able to multiply in infants. The toxin produced by these bacteria causes nervous-system paralysis that can lead to heart and respiratory failure.

Baby foods should be well tolerated, easily prepared, readily available, and inexpensive. Despite the fact that commercially prepared baby foods are nutritious and have no salt or sugar (except for some of the desserts), many parents choose to make their own baby foods. Before adding salt or seasoning to the family's dinner, use a baby food grinder to prepare a small amount of the meal for the baby. A blender is convenient for making larger amounts that can be put into ice cube trays. After they are frozen, the individual cubes can be popped into airtight bags, ready for quick thawing in a dish placed over a pan of simmering water. If you use commercially prepared baby food, read the labels carefully and try to stay away from "combination" foods or "dinners." They tend to be expensive and generally contain starch fillers that your baby doesn't need. Avoid desserts that are mostly sugar—they are a waste of money, have little nutritional value, and are bad for developing teeth.

By about nine months, when most babies have a few teeth and stronger jaw muscles, they are ready to practice feeding themselves. Finger foods such as toast, dry cereal, cheese, tofu, and banana chunks are good things for infants to practice on. Most babies are able to drink fairly well from a cup at this age and are beginning to show interest in spoons, although they are likely to be over a year old before they actually get the food all the way from the bowl into their mouths. Be prepared for mealtimes to be sloppy. A vinyl tablecloth under the highchair makes it easier to clean up. Eating, like crawling, walking, or any other complex skill, is learned through lots of practice.

After starting your baby on solid foods, add about six to eight ounces of water to your baby's daily diet. This will help to prevent constipation. As a rule of thumb, if your baby is consuming more than 48 ounces of formula per day, increase the solids.

How Much to Feed the Baby

Many parents are concerned about the correct amount to feed their infants. Start by giving solids once a day and gradually build up to three meals a day. A "serving" for a preschooler is roughly one tablespoon per year of the child's age (although this varies from one child to the next). General guidelines for a one-year-old's daily diet are as follows:

Milk: 16 to 24 ounces
Fruits and Vegetables: 4 servings, each 1 to 2 Tbsp. Vitamin
    C source—3 ounces daily. Vitamin A source—3 times
    weekly.
Breads and Cereals: 4 servings, each about ¼ the adult
    serving.
Meats, Poultry, Fish, Eggs: 2 servings, each about ½ ounce.

Keep in mind that children vary considerably with respect to how much they need to eat. Trying to "force" your child to eat more or less is not necessary. As long as you are offering nutritious foods, let your child's appetite be your guide.

Preventing Choking

Children can choke on almost any food, but they are most likely to have trouble with foods that are smooth, hard, slippery, and/or foods that are just the right size to plug the throat. The foods that cause the most problems are candy, peanuts and other nuts, grapes, hot dogs, popcorn, and hard pieces of fruits or vegetables.

The following are some guidelines for preventing choking in children under five years of age:

1. Never leave your child unattended when he or she is eating.

2. Because you may not have time for action when you are driving, don't allow children to eat in a car.

3. Cook foods well and cut them into small pieces, avoiding foods that the child is not yet capable of chewing. If you have doubts about a particular food, don't feed it to youngsters.

4. Don't allow children to drink from a cup or eat unless they're sitting up. Baby bottles should be held by a responsible person and not propped.

5. Remember that numbing topical teething anesthetics can interfere with the ability to swallow foods that require chewing.

6. Ask your pediatrician what to do if choking does occur.

7. Finally, don't worry excessively about the possibility of your baby choking. It is important for the baby to be exposed to a variety of tastes and textures of foods. Just make sure that you are present when he or she is eating, and use common sense in deciding what foods to offer.

Summing Up the Discussion

People have very strong views about nutrition and feeding solids and, much like discipline, it is an area in which our children's "performance" may seem to reflect our own adequacy or inadequacy as parents. Try to resist family and social pressures to start poor feeding habits such as introducing solids earlier than necessary, overfeeding, or offering sweets. Babies and small children know when they are full—don't force that last bite, push cleaning the plate, or play "flying it in." Avoid the tendency to offer children food in order to calm them down, distract them, or reward them.

Next week. The topic for next week's discussion has been left open. This gives us an opportunity to talk about some of the issues we still haven't touched on *(see Appendix 7.1 for some ideas to share with the group).* Next week will also be the last meeting of this class, so we will have to decide if we would like to continue getting together and, if so, make some plans for future meetings.

The author would like to acknowledge Beth Naylor, R.D., Lane Community College, for her contribution of material to this meeting.

Suggested Readings for Meeting #7

Eiger, Marvin S., M.D. and Olds, Sally Wendkos. *The Complete Book of Breastfeeding.* New York: Bantam, 1973.

Lansky, Vicki. *Feed Me, I'm Yours.* New York: Bantam, 1979.

First Foods for Infants

LINDA MORTON KNOTTS, R.D., M.P.H.

Lane Community College
Eugene, Oregon

Parents typically have a lot of questions when they begin teaching their baby to manage foods other than milk. Parents need to know when to introduce which foods, as well as how to prepare the food and how much to feed their child. Although this brief article cannot answer all of these questions, several charts have been provided to give parents some developmental and nutritional guidelines regarding first foods for infants. As with any chart listing "signs" or "goals" for infants, these charts are not to be interpreted as a rigid timetable that all normal children follow. Your child will develop in his or her own unique way.

Guideline for Starting Infants on Solid Foods

Approximate Age: 4 to 6 months

Food. Iron-fortified infant cereal. Begin with rice, barley, and oats. Later, introduce wheat.

227

Signs of readiness. Sits with support, opens mouth when food is coming; evidence of swallowing pattern; can transfer food from front to back of tongue.

How to. Mix cereal with breast milk, formula or evaporated milk; feed with a small spoon.

How much. Start with 1 tsp. and work up to ½ cup per day at one year of age.

Nutritional goal. To add iron to the infant's diet.

Developmental goal. To encourage coordination of the tongue and practice swallowing.

Approximate Age: 6 to 8 months

A. Food. Fruits and vegetables. Feed your infant a source of Vitamin C once per day, and a source of Vitamin A three or more times per week.

Signs of readiness. Already eating infant cereal.

How to. Clean, peel, and cook fresh or frozen fruits and vegetables and mash with a fork. Mash canned fruits with a fork (drain off syrup). Gradually work up to small chunks. Offer juice in a small cup.

How much. ¼ to ⅓ cup infant juice. Work up to a total of 4 to 8 Tbsp. solid food per day (divide into 1 to 2 Tbsp. servings).

Nutritional goal. To get your infant used to eating a variety of foods including good sources of Vitamins A and C.

Developmental goal. To encourage chewing, and expose the infant to lumpier foods of different textures and flavors.

B. Food. "Finger" breads and cereals (enriched and whole grain products).

Signs of readiness. Puts everything into his or her mouth, grabs at small objects.

How to. Allow infant to pick up and eat small strips, chunks, and "balls" of food.

How much. Will vary according to energy needs.

Nutritional goal. To add iron, B vitamins, trace minerals (in whole-grain products) and variety to diet.

Developmental goal. To encourage the development of pincer grasp and chewing skills.

Approximate Age: 7 to 10 months

A. Food. Meat and protein foods.

Signs of readiness. Evidence of "adult" chewing patterns, side-to-side movement with tongue, mashes food with jaws, up-and-down chewing movement.

How to. Modify texture of meat and other protein foods to match the infant's chewing abilities.

How much. Work up to 1 oz. total for the day.

Nutritional goal. To add protein to the diet as intake of breast milk or formula drops.

Developmental goal. To improve chewing skills.

B. Food. Table foods.

Signs of readiness. Sits in high-chair. Shows the ability and impulse to self-feed, shows good hand-to-mouth coordination and signs of palmar and pincer grasp.

How to. Have the infant join the family for meals. Progress from semisolid mashed foods to pieces of soft cooked foods. Allow some self-feeding.

Nutritional goal. To expand the variety of foods offered and make the transition from demand feeding that is typical of infants to the meal plus snack routine that is appropriate for toddlers.

Developmental goal. To learn social skills, improve pincer and palmar grasp, develop hand-eye coordination, and refine chewing and self-feeding skills.

Approximate Age: 10 to 12 months

Food. Weaning from milk.

Signs of readiness. Sits up with family at meals. Self-feeding is accomplished primarily by using his or her hands. Drinks with assistance from a cup.

How to. Talk with a doctor, nurse, or nutritionist about when and how to switch from breast milk or formula to pasteurized whole cow's milk.

How much. Varies from 16 to 24 oz. per day.

Nutritional goal. To eat a variety of solid foods from the four food groups (see next chart) in addition to milk, and work on establishing toddler-type eating routine.

Developmental goal. To continue promoting the development of biting, chewing, and swallowing, and improve self-feeding skills.

Four Food Groups for Infants

The following chart divides first foods for infants into the four food groups to help parents provide a nutritionally balanced diet for their infants. Don't give up if your child doesn't like a food the first time—it might take several tries over a period of years before he or she enjoys a certain food.

Protein Foods

Plain meats that are cooked and mashed: chicken, turkey, fish without bones, hamburger, juicy liver. You can make these moist by adding mashed vegetables, rice, macaroni, yogurt, broth, or milk.

Cooked egg yolk (add milk and mash together)
Cooked and then mashed dry beans
Cottage cheese
Cheese
Yogurt, plain
Puddings, custards (avoid the use of egg whites)

Breads and Cereals

Iron-fortified infant cereals
Breads (whole grain or enriched)
Macaroni, noodles, rice, millet, spaghetti, barley, bulgar
Rice cakes
Crackers
Pancakes

Milk

Breast milk or iron-fortified formula

0 to 2 months	18 to 20 oz. per day
3 to 6 months	24 to 32 oz. per day
6 to 12 months	16 to 32 oz. per day
1 year	16 to 24 oz. per day

Fruits and Vegetables

Vitamin C Sources
infant juices
cantaloupe
orange slices
spinach

Vitamin A Sources
winter squash
carrots
spinach
sweet potatoes
apricots
cantaloupe
pumpkin
plums (purple)

Other
white/red potatoes
green beans
green peas
beets
applesauce
pears
peaches

Finger Foods

cheese strips
tofu (soybean curd) strips
toast squares
cooked vegetable strips or slices
dry cereal pieces
rice cakes
soft cooked vegetables
soft pieces of fruit
crackers
strips of fruit or vegetable breads

Recommended Readings

Hinton, Sarah M., M.S., R.D. and Kerwin, Diane R., R.D., M.P.H. *Maternal, Infant, and Child Nutrition.* Chapel Hill, N.C.: Health Sciences Consortium, 1981.

Naylor, Beth, R.D., M.P.H. *First Foods for Infants.* Eugene, Oregon: Consumer-Homemaker Education Project, Lane Community College, 1982.

Satter, Ellyn, R.D. *Child of Mine: Feeding with Love and Good Sense.* Palo Alto, Calif.: Bull Publishing Company, 1983.

MEETING 8

Summing Up the Class

Goals

To discuss a topic that has been selected by the group and decide whether or not to continue meeting. This meeting has been left open to allow some flexibility in bringing the class to an end. It can be used as an opportunity to follow up previous topics with a guest speaker or further discussion, or to talk about new topics that interest group members (the agenda for this meeting should be selected at the end of meeting #7—see Appendix 7.1 for some suggestions).

Preliminaries. *Share everyone's news.*

Discussion

Topic and/or speaker selected by the group.

Summing Up the Class

The next order of business is to discuss the possibility of continuing to meet as a parent support group, now that the class is ending. Ask members of the group if they would like to continue getting together. If most of the group members indicate that they are interested, establish a time and a place for future meetings. Decide whether to assign the job of group coordinator to one person or rotate the responsibility among group members. Discuss the focus for the group—what are some of the topics that the group would like to discuss in more detail? If possible, write down some of the ideas the group generates and come up with a tentative plan for the next one or two meetings. Ask if there are any speakers in the community that the group would like to invite. Ask for a volunteer or two to bring snacks to the next meeting, and bring the meeting to an end.

If the group decides not to continue meeting it is important to bring the group to a sense of closure. Now is the time to deal with any loose ends such as fees to be collected, books loaned out, and questions that need to be answered. Make sure that all group members have a copy of the roster with everyone's name and address so that members will be able to stay in touch if they wish. If there are some members who would like to continue to belong to a support group, perhaps they could be referred to another Birth to Three group in the area. Finally, offer some concluding remarks that convey a positive outlook on parenting, and then end the meeting.

Suggested Readings for Meeting #8

Boston Women's Health Book Collective. *Ourselves and Our Children: A Book By and For Parents.* New York: Random House, 1978.

Kelly, Marguerite and Parsons, Elia. *The Mother's Almanac.* New York: Doubleday, 1975.

Sullivan, S. Adams. *The Father's Almanac.* New York: Doubleday, 1980.

Appendices

Appendix 4.1
Generic Flier

The flier that appears on the next page has been provided to make it easy for you to find other new parents who would like to belong to a Birth to Three group. All that you need to do is to photocopy the flier and write your name and telephone number in the spaces provided. The fliers can then be posted on bulletin boards at the local YMCA, YWCA, community centers, and other places that parents frequent.

Do you have an
INFANT or TODDLER?

Would you like to meet other new parents in your neighborhood to exchange ideas, share experiences, and learn about raising children?

Announcing
▬▬▬▬▬ Birth To Three: ▬▬▬▬▬
A Self-Help Program for New Parents

Birth To Three is a highly successful program that shows parents how to form discussion and support groups so that they can meet one another, and learn about childrearing together. The program is founded on the belief that parents are in a perfect position to help each other through the early childrearing years. Other parents understand what you are going through and can provide assistance, advice, and friendship at a critical time in the development of your family. This program has helped thousands of parents get off to a good start with their babies and toddlers. In a recent survey, parents in Birth To Three groups were asked if they would recommend the program to other parents—100% said they would!

A Birth To Three group is a place to go where the baby is welcome, and it offers an opportunity for fun and stimulation. It takes a special setting to discuss the issues that concern new parents most—a Birth To Three group is that special setting.

A New Discussion Group is Being Organized Now!

For more information, call _____ and ask for _____.
                               (phone #)   (name of organizer)

Parents Helping Other Parents to Learn About Raising Children

Appendix 4.2
Sample Letter

Dear Parent,

Would you like to meet other parents with infants living in your neighborhood?

As parents of young children, we know that being with a baby can be both delightful and frustrating, rewarding and irritating. Many times, each of us has wished for the company of other parents with infants who understand what we are going through.

We have joined together to form Birth to Three, a program of support services to parents of small children. We organize neighborhood groups where parents can share ideas, make friends, see other babies the same age as theirs, discuss the topics that concern them, and learn together. One of us will be calling you soon to invite you to a meeting.

We offer a free, attractive poster listing the services that are available to parents of young kids in the Eugene-Springfield area. The poster also suggests a number of worthwhile books on parenting and child development that can be obtained at the library.

If you'd like to talk to someone about the feelings you're having as a parent, we're available by phone, or we can arrange to visit you at home if you would prefer. Even if you're not having problems with your baby, but just need information about the services available in this area, please feel comfortable about calling anytime at 484-4401.

If you know of other parents with infants who might also be interested in the Birth to Three program, let them know about us!

Hope to be seeing you,

Appendix 5.1
Topics for Discussion in Toddler Groups

Inside the World of the Toddler

- the stages of physical, emotional, and intellectual development
- the toddler's "tasks"
- differences in temperament between toddlers

Discipline

- encouraging cooperation
- how to establish firm and fair limits
- ways to deal with temper tantrums, biting, hitting, and destructiveness
- using threats, bribes, and other circular routes
- spanking, time out, and other approaches to discipline

How to Talk So Your Children Will Listen

- the importance of finding the "words that work" and saying them clearly and with respect

Sleep Issues

- naps, bedtime rituals
- "up in the middle of the nighters"
- dreams and nightmares
- the family bed

Fearfulness and Anxiety

- exploring our children's fears and our own as parents
- helping children overcome extreme shyness
- understanding stuttering problems
- the physical risks faced by toddlers
- protecting our children and overprotectiveness

Co-Parenting

- what do we want from our partners as parents?
- ways to develop cooperation
- issues involved in single parenting
- special concerns in blended families
- setting some family goals

Sex Role Differences

- observing our boys and girls and the fascinating differences between them
- what are some of our responses as parents to sex role development?

Balancing Our Own Lives and Roles

- the myth of "supermom/superwoman"
- is time management a bad joke?

Appendix 6.1
Sample Questionnaire

We've been requested by some of the agencies that fund us to ask people participating in groups what they think of Birth to Three. Could you help us by answering these questions? Please don't sign your name—we want to keep this anonymous. Feel free to use the reverse side of the page if you have additional comments.

1. What were your goals in coming to Birth to Three?

2. Do you feel that your goals have been met?
   _____ yes _____ no
   Comments?

3. How many children do you have? _____
   What are their ages? _____

4. Have you ever belonged to a Birth to Three group before? _____ yes _____ no

5. Do you have friends with small children living in the area (not from your Birth to Three group)?
   _____ yes _____ no

6. Do you have relatives in the area? _____ yes _____ no
   If so, do they help with child care? _____ yes _____ no

7. Would you recommend Birth to Three to other parents?
   _____ yes _____ no

8. Do you feel that you are a better parent as a result of being in a Birth to Three group? _____ yes _____ no
   Comments?

9. Birth to Three's purpose is to bring parents together so that they can share information and give support to each other. What have you gained from your Birth to Three group? (please check all that apply)

____ information   ____ friendship

____ support   ____ technical help (babysitting, help with transportation, etc.)

     ____ other (please specify)

10. What sorts of information did you need as a new parent? (please check all that apply)

____ general health   ____ developmental stages

____ nutrition   of children

     ____ other (please specify)

11. Do you read the Birth to Three newsletter?

____ yes ____ no

If so, would you recommend it to other parents?

____ yes ____ no

12. Did you know that you could call Birth to Three just to talk if you were having a rough day with your child?

____ yes ____ no

Have you ever called on such a day? ____ yes ____ no

If so, did it help?

13. Do you have a Birth to Three poster? ____ yes ____ no

If so, do you find it useful? ____ yes ____ no

14. Have you ever attended any lectures in Birth to Three's "special events" series? ____ yes ____ no

If so, were they worthwhile? ____ yes ____ no

15. How is being a new parent different from what you expected?

16. What are the major areas of stress in your life now that you are a new parent?
     _____ fatigue
    _____ financial strain
    _____ lack of communication with partner
    _____ not enough time to myself
    _____ the baby
    _____ the baby's sibling(s)
    _____ other (please describe)

17. What additional services would you like to see Birth to Three offer?

18. Do you feel that your tax money should be spent to support programs like Birth to Three? _____ yes _____ no

* * * * * * * * * * * *

We'd like to have some idea about the background of people coming to Birth to Three groups. Again, this questionnaire is anonymous.

19. Education (please circle the highest grade you have completed)
    Grade 1 2 3 4 5 6 7 8 9 10 11 12
    College 1 2 3 4 5 6

20. Family income:
    _____ under $10,000 a year
    _____ $10,000–$20,000 a year
    _____ over $20,000 a year

21. Are you a single parent? _____ yes _____ no

22. Your age:
_____ under 20 _____ 20–29 _____ 30–39 _____ over 40

Many, many thanks. We really appreciate your help.

Appendix 7.1
Suggested Topics for Group Discussions

What did you do before your baby was born?

Share your birth experiences.

Regaining your health and strength after birth: rest, nutrition, exercise.

How to deal with isolation and boredom without taking it out on your kids.

Adjustment: how to handle stress, learning to relax.

How to be more efficient with your time.

Nursing/bottle feeding.

Nutrition: how and when to introduce solids.

First aid in emergency situations.

What are the alternatives for family planning? (A nurse, physician or speaker from Planned Parenthood could be invited to talk about the various methods of birth control.)

Contrast your expectations of babies and parenthood with the reality.

The "ideal" mother/father: what are her/his attributes?

How do you view your role as a parent? What are your hopes for your child? How would you like your child to regard you?

How do you see parental roles changing? In your household what sort of division of labor exists between you and your partner in work and child care?

How has your relationship with your partner changed since the baby?

Fathers: are they participating/not participating in baby care?

Working at a career vs. staying at home: how do you regard "mothering," as a job, profession or drudgery?

Society's stereotypes about motherhood: how do they make you feel? Respected, guilty, inadequate?

How does the feminist movement affect you as a mother?

How do you reconcile paid/unpaid work outside the home with childrearing?

How were you raised? How has your upbringing affected you and your style of raising your own children? How has having a baby affected your relationship with your own mother?

Have your relations with parents, in-laws, and friends changed since the birth of your baby?

Now that you are a parent, do you view your neighborhood or community differently?

"Bloopers" you've made with your baby.

Crying infants: what crying means and how to respond to it.

Individual differences in infants: discuss the issue of infant temperament.

Baby-proofing the house.

Infant development: motor, emotional, cognitive.

Language development.

How to get along with toddlers: viewing your toddler positively.

Discipline for children under three: review some different approaches.

Helping siblings adjust to the new baby.

Sibling rivalry.

Developing feelings of independence and security in your children.

What are your expectations of your kids?

Toys (Bring a toy that your baby likes. Discuss the toys and what constitutes a good toy at different ages.)

Consumerism: teaching kids about money.

TV: uses and misuses.

Games, songs, finger-plays that are appropriate for different ages.

Car seat safety.

Babysitters: how to train them.

Babysitting exchanges, co-ops, play groups.

Child-care alternatives and how to decide which one is appropriate for you and your children. What to look for in a good nursery school.

How to stimulate kids to learn without pressuring them.

Daughters and sons: do you treat them differently, and do you have different expectations for their behavior?

Children's books (bring some of your favorite books to share with the group).

Raising two kids under the age of three.

Sex education: how was the topic dealt with by your own parents? How do you want to teach your children?

Single parenting.

Step-parenting.

Adopting a child.

Raising a handicapped child.

Importance of preparing a will and naming a legal guardian for your child.

Information on community resources.

The group can choose a book that everyone will read and discuss.

The group can do a handicraft project together; for example, make a mobile or learn to sew pants for young children.

Appendix 7.2
Finger-Plays and Action Songs

FIVE LITTLE MONKEYS

Five little monkeys sitting in a tree, teasing Mr. Alligator,
"You can't catch me! You can't catch me!"
Along came Mr. Alligator quiet as can be.
SNAP! (Clap)
Four little monkeys. . . .
Three little monkeys. . . .
Two little monkeys. . . .
One little monkey. . . .

WHERE IS THUMBKIN?

Where is Thumbkin? Where is Thumbkin?
    Here I am. Here I am.
How are you today sir? Very well, I thank you.
    Run away. Run away.
Where is Pointer? . . . .
Where is Middleman? . . . .
Where is Ringman? . . . .
Where is Pinky? . . . .
Where is the Whole Family? . . . .

CLIP, CLOP HORSIE

Clip clop horsie on your way.
We've been together for many a day.
So when your tail goes swish,
and the wheels go round,
Getty-up, getty-up, we're homeward bound.

BUMBLE BEE

I'm bringing home a baby bumble bee.
Won't my mommy be so proud of me?
Cuz I'm bringing home a baby bumble bee.
Buzzy, buzzy, buzzy, OUCH!
He stung me!

FIVE LITTLE CHICKADEES

Five little chickadees peeping at the door;
　　One flew away and then there were four.
Four little chickadees sitting in a tree;
　　One flew away and then there were three.
Three little chickadees looking at you;
　　One flew away and then there were two.
Two little chickadees sitting in the sun;
　　One flew away and then there was one.
One little chickadee left all alone;
　　One flew away and then there were none.

BUS SONG

The *wheels* on the bus go round and round; round and
　　round; round and round. The wheels on the bus
　　go round and round all through the town.
The *windows* on the bus go up and down, etc.
The *doors* on the bus go open and shut, etc.
The *money* on the bus goes clink, clink, clink, etc.
The *wipers* on the bus go swish, swish, swish, etc.
The *lights* on the bus go blink, blink, blink, etc.
The *baby* on the bus goes hi, hi, hi, etc.
The *Mommy* on the bus goes kiss, kiss, kiss, etc.
The *Daddy* on the bus goes hug, hug, hug, etc.
The *people* on the bus go up and down, etc.
The *driver* on the bus says move on back, etc.
The *horn* on the bus goes beep, beep, beep, etc.

OPEN, SHUT THEM

Open, shut them; open, shut them. Give your hands a clap.
Open, shut them; open, shut them. Put them in your lap.
Creep them, creep them, creep them, creep them right up
    to your chin.
Open up your little mouth, but do not let them in.

HAPPY AND YOU KNOW IT

If you're happy and you know it, clap your hands.
If you're happy and you know it, clap your hands.
If you're happy and you know it, then your face will
    surely show it.
If you're happy and you know it, clap your hands.
If you're mad and you know it, stomp your feet. Etc.
If you're tired and you know it, rub your eyes. Etc.

ITSY BITSY SPIDER (or EENSY BEENSY)

The itsy bitsy spider went up the water spout;
Down came the rain and washed the spider out!
Out came the sun and dried up all the rain,
And the itsy bitsy spider went up the spout again.

TEAPOT

I'm a little teapot, short and stout,
Here is my handle and here is my spout,
When I get all steamed up then I shout
Just tip me over and pour me out!

APPLE TREE

Way up high in the apple tree,
Two little apples were smiling at me;
I shook that tree as hard as I could;
Down came the apples, and ummm, they were good.

Repeat with oranges, lemons (sour), or anything.

WHERE IS BABY?

Where is X where, where;
Where is X where, where?
Where is X where, where;
Where is X where, where?
Is he up on the mountain? No. No.
Is he down at the fountain? No. No.
Is he outside playing? No. No.
Where is X? Here. Here.
X, X, X. (Clap out each syllable of child's name).
X = *child's name*

Appendix 7.3
24-Hour Sleeping, Feeding, and Crying Diary

Baby's Name _____ Date _____

The following charts have been designed to help parents keep track of the sleeping, feeding, and crying behavior of their infants. This chart was developed by Mary K. Rothbart, Ph.D., Infant Temperament Project, Department of Psychology, University of Oregon. Reprinted by permission.

Below are listed 15-minute intervals for a full 24-hour period. Please write in:

S for any time period when the baby was sleeping.
W when the baby was awake but not eating or crying.
E when the baby was eating.
C when the baby was crying.

If the baby did more than one of these things in an interval, write the letters for each activity. An activity does not need to fill the entire interval for you to write it in. Write down the letter for an activity if it occurs at all in the interval. Note that whenever you write in E or C, writing W is unnecessary.

6:00-6:14 a.m.	2:00-2:14 p.m.	10:00-10:14 p.m.
6:15-6:29	2:15-2:29	10:15-10:29
6:30-6:44	2:30-2:44	10:30-10:44
6:45-6:59	2:45-2:59	10:45-10:59
7:00-7:14	3:00-3:14	11:00-11:14
7:15-7:29	3:15-3:29	11:15-11:29
7:30-7:44	3:30-3:44	11:30-11:44
7:45-7:59	3:45-3:59	11:45-11:59
8:00-8:14	4:00-4:14	12:00-12:14 a.m.
8:15-8:29	4:15-4:29	12:15-12:29
8:30-8:44	4:30-4:44	12:30-12:44
8:45-8:59	4:45-4:59	12:45-12:59
9:00-9:14	5:00-5:14	1:00-1:14
9:15-9:29	5:15-5:29	1:15-1:29
9:30-9:44	5:30-5:44	1:30-1:44
9:45-9:59	5:45-5:59	1:45-1:59
10:00-10:14	6:00-6:14	2:00-2:14
10:15-10:29	6:15-6:29	2:15-2:29
10:30-10:44	6:30-6:44	2:30-2:44
10:45-10:59	6:45-6:59	2:45-2:59
11:00-11:14	7:00-7:14	3:00-3:14
11:15-11:29	7:15-7:29	3:15-3:29
11:30-11:44	7:30-7:44	3:30-3:44
11:45-11:59	7:45-7:59	3:45-3:59
12:00-12:14 p.m.	8:00-8:14	4:00-4:14
12:15-12:29	8:15-8:29	4:15-4:29
12:30-12:44	8:30-8:44	4:30-4:44
12:45-12:59	8:45-8:59	4:45-4:59
1:00-1:14	9:00-9:14	5:00-5:14
1:15-1:29	9:15-9:29	5:15-5:29
1:30-1:44	9:30-9:44	5:30-5:44
1:45-1:59	9:45-9:59	5:45-5:59

About the Author

Andi Fischhoff received her Master's Degree in Early Childhood and Special Education from the Hebrew University of Jerusalem in 1974. While working on her degree, she became involved in counseling families and developing early intervention programs for babies with developmental problems. In 1978, she co-founded Birth to Three in Eugene, Oregon, along with Sue Kelly and Minalee Saks. Currently, she is the Assistant Director in charge of fundraising.

Andi and her husband, Baruch, have three children: Maya (age 14), Ilya (age 8), and Noam (age 1½). When Noam was born in the summer of 1984, Andi finally had a chance to become a member of a Birth to Three group (she had been a group facilitator many times, but not a group member). "I was eager to see what it would be like, and I'm impressed. The group really 'works.' It's supportive, caring, practical, and fun—something like a large family. And I truly needed it as much as the next person."

Index to
Annotated Reading
List Categories

Annotated Reading List

This reading list has been put together to give parents and group leaders a place to start looking for more information on a particular topic. These are the books and magazines that group members have found most useful and that have been most helpful in facilitating group discussions. The annotated reading list has been divided into the categories listed on the opposite page to make it easier to find materials of interest. We have also organized the same reading list alphabetically by author. There are many excellent books available—these are a few of the ones that we would like to recommend.

The Transition to Parenthood

Boston Women's Health Book Collective. *Ourselves and Our Children: A Book By and For Parents*. New York: Random House, 1978. 276 pages. $6.95

Here is a wonderful book by the authors of *Our Bodies, Ourselves* about the many varied expressions of parenthood. There are sections on becoming a parent, being a parent during the beginning, middle, teenage, and grown-up years, society's impact on parents, and the different forms families take. This is a book to come back to again and again; it is enriched by the observations of hundreds of parents whose comments elaborate the narrative.

Jaffe, Sandra S. and Viertel, Jack. *Becoming Parents: Preparing for the Emotional Changes of First-Time Parenthood.* New York: Atheneum Press, 1979. $11.95

This book focuses on the psychological and emotional aspects of the parents' adjustment to the new baby. By interviewing hundreds of new parents and presenting in-depth interviews with six couples, the authors explore the many changes parents undergo in integrating the new baby into their lives. This is a very readable and worthwhile book.

Rozdilsky, Mary Lou and Banet, Barbara. *What Now? A Handbook for New Parents.* New York: Scribner, rev. ed., 1975. 164 pages. $3.95

An excellent book with good, basic information about nutrition, exercise, and parentcare. It is a guide to help parents make a positive emotional transition to parenthood.

Basic Health and Child Development

Ames, Louise Bates, Ilg, F.L., and Haber, C.C. *Your One-Year-Old.* New York: Delta, 1982. 167 pages. $5.95

This is an extremely thorough and intelligent discussion of the period between the child's first and second birthdays. It is part of a series from the Gesell Institute, which already includes *Your Two-Year-Old, Your Three-Year-Old, Your Four-Year-Old, Your Five-Year-Old,* and *Your Six-Year Old.* Topics covered range from general characteristics of

258

this age, the child's accomplishments and abilities, what the world looks like to a one-year-old, and techniques parents can use with infants during this period.

Brazelton, T. Berry. *Infants and Mothers: Differences in Development.* New York: Dell, rev. ed., 1983. 302 pages. $10.95

In this revised version, Dr. Brazelton introduces new material on recent research findings in neonatology and addresses some of the contemporary issues facing parents. As in the first edition, he describes the developmental histories of three very different infants to demonstrate how broad the range of normal development can be. This is an important and very readable book.

Cheldelin, Larry V. *Your Baby's Secret World.* Brookline Village, Mass.: Brandon Press, 1983. 167 pages. $6.50

Written by a pediatrician, this book is concise, practical preparation for tackling the tasks of parenting an infant from birth through three years of age. The material is divided into four sections: "Preparing for your Baby," "The New Arrival," "Growth and Development," and "Health and Well Being." It offers sound information about well-child care, illness, feeding, crying, toilet training, and discipline, and ready answers to questions parents typically ask their pediatricians.

Leach, Penelope. *Your Baby and Child: From Birth to Age Five.* New York: Knopf, 1978. 512 pages. $11.95

This is an outstanding guide to child care and development. Encyclopedic in scope, it deals thoroughly and readably with the physical and psychological development of the child from birth through the preschool age. This book is definitely recommended.

Princeton Center for Infancy. *The Parenting Advisor.* Frank Caplan, Ed. New York: Anchor, 1978. 551 pages. $12.95

This is an extremely thorough book integrating material from physicians, psychologists, and parents on all areas of childrearing—from health and nutrition to the social, sensory, and emotional development of the child. This book is highly recommended.

Spock, Benjamin. *Baby and Child Care.* New York: Pocket Books, rev. ed., 1976. 666 pages. $4.95

A classic, Dr. Spock's basic book on child care remains a worthwhile addition to every parent's library. Easy to read, reassuring in tone, it offers sound guidelines in areas such as feeding, scheduling, disciplining, handling childhood illnesses, and bringing up kids in these turbulent times. The special issues involved in caring for twins and premature and handicapped babies are also discussed.

Practical Parenting Books

Kelly, Marguerite and Parsons, Elia. *The Mother's Almanac.* New York: Doubleday, 1975. 288 pages. $5.95

A great book on living with children under six years of age, it is full of the warm-hearted and entertaining wisdom of two very experienced mothers. It covers topics such as child-proofing the house, toilet training, teaching manners, second children, health hazards, and a great deal more.

Sullivan, S. Adams. *The Father's Almanac.* New York: Doubleday, 1980. 342 pages. $11.95

A complement to *The Mother's Almanac,* this is another excellent offering, loaded with insights and practical information on expectant fathers, baby care, work, families, everyday and special events, teaching discipline, and working and playing with kids.

Emotional Needs of Children and Parents

Briggs, Dorothy Corkille. *Your Child's Self-Esteem*. New York: Doubleday Dolphin, 1975. 334 pages. $6.95

A book to balance the volumes on children's intellectual and physical development, this one instructs us on nurturing our children's emotional health. The author has some very valuable things to say about fostering a sense of self-worth in children from infancy to late adolescence. This is a wonderful book.

Fraiberg, Selma H. *The Magic Years: Understanding and Handling the Problems of Early Childhood*. New York: Scribner, 1959. 302 pages. $5.95

Although originally published 25 years ago, this book is still very much worth reading. It is a psychoanalytically oriented account of personality development during the first five years of life with a discussion of some of the typical problems that emerge with each developmental stage.

Leboyer, Frederick. *Loving Hands: The Traditional Indian Art of Baby Massaging*. New York: Knopf, 1976. 136 pages. $10.95

A baby massage manual, written by the French physician who wrote *Birth Without Violence*.

McBride, Angela Barron. *The Growth and Development of Mothers*. New York: Harper & Row, 1973. 150 pages. $4.95

Society's expectations of mothers, and the expectations mothers place on themselves, their husbands, and their children are the substance of this book. The author makes some very important points about the developmental needs of parents during the various phases of their children's growth and how to stave off the feelings of depression, guilt, and anger that commonly besiege parents.

Thevenin, Tine. *The Family Bed.* Minneapolis, Minn.: self-published, 1976. 195 pages. $4.95

An interesting book that challenges the social taboo regarding children sleeping with their parents.

Cognitive and Motor Development

Caplan, Frank and Theresa. *The Second Twelve Months of Life.* New York: Grosset & Dunlap, 1977. 305 pages. $9.95

A clear, understandable, and well-organized guide to cognitive and motor development, language acquisition, and emerging social skills. This book is a continuation of The Princeton Center for Infancy and Early Childhood's *The First Twelve Months of Life.*

Developmental Language and Speech Center. *Teach Your Child to Talk.* Grand Rapids, Mich.: CEBCO Standard Pub., 1975. 145 pages. $1.50

This book describes normal speech and language development, answers parents' questions about development, and suggests enjoyable activities for parents of preschoolers that will facilitate good speech and language development.

Levy, Janine. *The Baby Exercise Book: For the First Fifteen Months.* New York: Pantheon, 1975. 127 pages. $6.95

This book offers parents and educators exercises to encourage the development of self-awareness in infants and very young children through movement. The exercises are suitable for the baby's first 15 months and photographs make the suggestions easy to follow. The author is a French physician whose special interest is infant physical development.

Princeton Center for Infancy and Early Childhood. *The First Twelve Months of Life.* Frank Caplan, Ed. New York: Grosset & Dunlap, 1973. 252 pages. $9.95

This is a month-by-month review of the child's first year, with considerable reference to the research literature in the area of infant development. More scholarly than most other books that guide parents, it is both interesting and very useful in helping parents sensitively interpret some of the mysteries of infant behavior.

White, Burton L. *The First Three Years of Life.* New York: Avon, 1975. 275 pages. $4.95

This is an excellent, informative guide for enhancing a child's educational development during the first three years. The author strongly maintains, with considerable scientific support, that these are the years in which parents can exercise the most influence on their child's future intellectual and social skills. The 36 months are divided into seven phases. General behavior, educational and social development, and recommended toys and childrearing practices—as well as those the author does not recommend—are presented for each phase. This book is definitely worth reading.

Toys, Games, and Creative Learning Activities for Children

Burtt, Kent Garland and Kalkstein, Karen. *Smart Toys: A Parent's Guide to Quality Time with Preschoolers.* New York: Harper Colophon, 1981. 167 pages. $8.95

This book describes the baby's abilities during six stages of growth and suggests educational play experiences for each of those stages. The toys are inexpensive, easy to construct (there are simple line drawings showing how the toys are made) and they don't require any special crafts abilities or materials.

Kraus, Charles and Linda. *Charles the Clown's Guide to Children's Parties*. Rolling Hills Estates, Calif.: Jalmar Press, 1983. 294 pages. $9.95

This is one of the best books around on the subject of parties. With sensitivity, humor, and imagination, the authors (a professional children's entertainer and an early childhood specialist) have written an extremely useful guide to successfully organizing kids' parties. Sections are included on planning the event, games for every age, craft activities, dramatic play, excursions, foods, and party favors.

Marzollo, Jean. *Supertot: Creative Learning Activities for Children One to Three and Sympathetic Advice for Their Parents*. New York: Harper Colophon, 1977. 152 pages. $3.95.

This book is delightful. It contains some very good thoughts on living happily with young kids, finding things to do together (including making toys and dabbling in art and music), and coping with the inevitable hassles. There is a section on starting a play group as well as pointers on topics such as how to carry off a successful birthday party and endure rainy days.

Marzollo, Jean and Lloyd, Janice. *Learning Through Play*. New York: Harper Colophon, 1972. 204 pages. $3.95

A wonderful, easy-to-read, and easy-to-use book for any parent of a preschooler, it contains many excellent suggestions for games and other learning activities. The book is divided into eleven sections including sensory development, language development, pre-reading, sorting and classifying, counting and measuring, and problem solving. Many of the activities can be used with small groups of children as well as with one child.

Painter, Genevieve. *Teach Your Baby.* New York: Simon & Schuster, 1971. 223 pages. $8.95

Written by another authority on infant and preschool education, this book presents a program of daily activities that parents and children can enjoy together and that are geared for stages of development from infancy through four years of age.

Discipline and Childrearing Primers

Ames, Louise Bates with Haber, Carol Chase and the Gesell Institute of Human Development. *He Hit Me First: When Brothers and Sisters Fight.* New York: Dembner Books, 1982. 181 pages. $7.95

Here is an interesting book about a problem that, at one time or another, plagues most households with more than one child. "Why do children fight? The answer may come as a surprise. They do it because they enjoy it and it gives them something to do. Another reason is that nearly all children are competing desperately for their parent's approval, love, and attention." This is a useful and recommended book.

Baruch, Dorothy Walter. *New Ways in Discipline.* New York: McGraw-Hill, 1949. 268 pages. $12.95

This is a wonderful, warm, and compassionate book that is as valid today as when it was written 35 years ago. There are some marvelous truths here, and any parent would find this worth reading and re-reading.

Crary, Elizabeth. *Without Spanking or Spoiling: A Practical Approach to Toddler and Preschool Guidance.* Seattle, Wash.: Parenting Press, 1979. 192 pages. $6.95

This is an excellent book which presents information from several different approaches to child guidance (discipline): Parent Effectiveness Training, Behavior Modification, Transactional Analysis, and the Adlerian-Dreikurs approach. Examples and exercises illustrate the use of these techniques with small children.

Dreikurs, Rudolph. *Children: The Challenge.* New York: Hawthorn Books, 1964. 330 pages. $6.95

An intelligent approach to discipline and family life, this book advocates use of democratic methods and avoidance of power struggles. Definitely worth reading, although the discussion may be more appropriate for parents with pre-schoolers and school-aged kids than for parents with infants and toddlers.

Faber, Adele and Mazlish, Elaine. *How to Talk So Kids Will Listen and Listen So Kids Will Talk.* New York: Avon, 1980. 233 pages. $4.95

The authors lead parenting workshops based on the work of the late child psychologist Dr. Haim Ginott. Their book has much practical advice (with helpful exercises and assignments) for parents who want to nag their children less, find alternatives to punishment, and help their children feel better about themselves.

Ginott, Haim G. *Between Parent and Child.* New York: McMillan, 1956. 201 pages. $3.50

This is a classic and should be read by every parent. Topics covered include communicating with children, ways of praising and criticizing, avoiding self-defeating patterns, discipline, responsibility, and independence.

Lerman, Saf. *Parent Awareness*. Minneapolis, Minn.: Winston Press, 1980. 252 pages. $7.95

Written in clear, simple language, this book is full of sensible and useful information. In a question and answer format, using situations parents routinely confront, the author discusses discipline, children's fears, independence, talking about sex, death, and divorce. She emphasizes the importance of humor and flexibility in dealing with children and has some extremely worthwhile things to say about discipline, the shortcomings of physical punishment, and alternative strategies.

Patterson, Gerald R. *Living with Children*. Champaign, Ill.: Research Press, rev. ed., 1976. 114 pages. $8.95

This book offers a practical approach to dealing with children's misbehavior through a social learning perspective. The ideas are easy to use and understand and can be applied to common behavior problems such as children's teasing, toilet training three-year-olds, bed-wetting, temper tantrums, whining, and resisting bedtime.

Weiss, Joan Soloman. *Your Second Child*. New York: Summit Books, 1981. 277 pages. $8.95

This book addresses many of the questions parents encounter when they consider having, or care for, a second child. The author discusses the implications of spacing, dealing with the physical and psychological aspects of a second pregnancy, birth-order effects, preparing the first child for the second, sibling rivalry, and scheduling and freeing time for the parents.

Nutrition

Eiger, Marvin S. and Olds, Sally Wendkos. *The Complete Book of Breastfeeding*. New York: Bantam, 1973. 193 pages. $2.95

Good, complete, and unbiased advice to help mothers succeed at breastfeeding.

La Leche League International. *The Womanly Art of Breastfeeding*. Franklin Park, Ill.: self-published, rev. ed., 1981. 358 pages. $7.95

The authoritative guide to breastfeeding.

Lansky, Vicki. *Feed Me, I'm Yours*. New York: Bantam, 1974. 153 pages. $2.95

This book has lots of practical advice and recipes for homemade, natural babyfood, finger foods, toddler foods, snacks, and kitchen fun. This book is definitely recommended.

Medical Guides

Boston Children's Medical Center. *Child Health Encyclopedia*. Richard I. Feinbloom, Ed. New York: Dell, 1978. 608 pages. $9.95

An exhaustive guide to well- and sick-child care.

Green, Martin I. *A Sigh of Relief*. New York: Bantam, 1977. $12.95

An excellent book on coping with medical emergencies, it begins with sections on child safety and preventing accidents, then gives concise, easy-to-follow instructions for handling injuries if they do occur.

Fathers

Parke, Ross D. *Fathers*. Cambridge, Mass.: Harvard University Press, 1981. 115 pages. $3.95

An excellent book, it reviews the research pertaining to fathers' interactions with their children and the ways in which they influence their children's development. The discussion begins with the expectant father and also deals with the special circumstances of divorce and custody, step-fathers, and husbands.

Two-Career Families

Norris, Gloria and Miller, JoAnn. *The Working Mother's Complete Handbook: Everything You Need to Know to Succeed on the Job and at Home*. New York: Dutton, 1979. 304 pages. $9.95

A good resource for families in which both parents are trying to juggle the demands of careers and family life.

Single Parents

Atlas, Stephen L. *Single Parenting*. Englewood Cliffs, N.J.: Prentice-Hall, 1981. 234 pages. $5.95

The author is a past president of Parents Without Partners. There is a lot of information here about community organizations and counseling resources, and advice on how to create a positive family structure that meets the needs of the children as well as the single parent.

Galper, Miriam. *Co-Parenting: Sharing Your Child Equally.* Philadelphia, Penn.: Running Press, 1978. 150 pages.

A source book for the separated or divorced family. A social worker and also a divorced parent, Ms. Galper describes the system known as joint custody worked out by many parents as an alternative to the more traditional forms of custody. In this system, both parents continue to assume an equal role in their child's upbringing, maintaining a close relationship with that child, despite the dissolution of the marriage.

Klein, Carole. *The Single Parent Experience*. New York: Avon, 1973. 300 pages. $2.50

A good book, containing material drawn from the author's interviews with more than 200 single parents. Topics include the male single parent, homosexual parents, adoptive parents, the social realities of being a single parent, and the psychological effects of having a single parent.

Teaching Children About Sex

Bernstein, Ann. *The Flight of the Stork*. New York: Dell, 1980. 218 pages.

Reporting on her interviews with over 100 children, the author advises parents on how they can talk with their children about sex and reproduction in ways that their children will understand.

Non-Sexist Childrearing

Pogrebin, Letty Cottin. *Growing Up Free: Raising Your Child in the 80's*. New York: Bantam, 1980. 640 pages. $8.95

Ms. Pogrebin is a founder of *Ms.* magazine and continues to write for *Ms.* She also served as a consultant on the *Free to be, You and Me* book, record, and TV special. Her book is full of advice to parents on how they can help their chil-

270

dren to achieve their full potential. This is a non-sexist guide to childrearing that is worth reading.

Grandparents

Dodson, Fitzhugh with Reuben, Paula. *How to Grandparent.* New York: Harper & Row, 1981. 372 pages. $6.95

A very readable book, it is filled with useful and positive suggestions that will nurture the relationship between grandparents, child, and parents. The focus is on the role and function of grandparents and on improving communication across generations. Special aspects of grandparenting including being a long-distance grandparent, visiting, gift giving, divorce, and the single-parent family are also discussed.

Magazines and Journals

Sometimes, when one is awfully busy, the notion of reading a book seems ludicrous. At such times, reading a magazine may be a better way to gather some new ideas and relax for a few minutes. There are some fine magazines for parents on the market. *Parents' Magazine* and *Working Mother* are obvious places to start, and these can be found at most newsstands. Other recommended journals and newsletters are:

Family Journal
RD2, Box 165
Putney, VT 05346

The Growing Child
22 N. Second St.
Lafayette, IN 47902

La Leche League News
La Leche League International
9616 Minneapolis Ave.
Franklin Park, IL 60131

Mothering
P.O. Box 2208
Albuquerque, NM 87103

Practical Parenting
18318 Minnetonka Blvd.
Deephaven, MN 55391

Books in Annotated Reading List Alphabetized by Author

Note: The category in which each book appears in the annotated reading list is given in parentheses.

Ames, Louise Bates with Haber, Carol Chase and the Gesell Institute of Human Development. *He Hit Me First.* (Discipline and Childrearing Primers)

Ames, Louis Bates, Ilg, F.L., and Haber, C.C. *Your One-Year-Old.* (Basic Health and Child Development)

Atlas, Stephen L. *Single Parenting.* (Single Parents)

Baruch, Dorothy Walter. *New Ways in Discipline.* (Discipline and Childrearing Primers)

Bernstein, Ann. *The Flight of the Stork.* (Teaching Children about Sex)

Boston Children's Medical Center. *Child Health Encyclopedia.* Richard I. Feinbloom, Ed. (Medical Guides)

Boston Women's Health Collective. *Ourselves and Our Children.* (Transition to Parenthood)

Brazelton, T. Berry. *Infants and Mothers.* (Basic Health and Child Development)

Briggs, Dorothy Corkille. *Your Child's Self-Esteem.* (Emotional Needs of Children and Parents)

Burtt, Kent Garland and Kalkstein, Karen. *Smart Toys.* (Toys, Games, and Creative Learning Activities for Children)

Caplan, Frank and Theresa. *The Second Twelve Months of Life.* (Cognitive and Motor Development)

Cheldelin, Larry V. *Your Baby's Secret World.* (Basic Health and Child Development)

Crary, Elizabeth. *Without Spanking or Spoiling.* (Discipline and Childrearing Primers)

Developmental Language and Speech Center. *Teach Your Child to Talk.* (Cognitive and Motor Development)

Dodson, Fitzhugh with Reuben, Paula. *How to Grandparent.* (Grandparents)

Dreikurs, Rudolph. *Children the Challenge.* (Discipline and Childrearing Primers)

Eiger, Marvin S. and Olds, Sally Wendkos. *The Complete Book of Breastfeeding.* (Nutrition)

Faber, Adele and Mazlish, Elaine. *How to Talk So Kids Will Listen and Listen So Kids Will Talk.* (Discipline and Childrearing Primers)

Fraiberg, Selma H. *The Magic Years.* (Emotional Needs of Children and Parents)

Galper, Miriam. *Co-Parenting.* (Single Parents)

Ginott, Haim G. *Between Parent and Child.* (Discipline and Childrearing Primers)

Green, Martin I. *A Sigh of Relief.* (Medical Guides)

Jaffe, Sandra S. and Viertel, Jack. *Becoming Parents.* (The Transition to Parenthood)

Kelly, Marguerite and Parsons, Elia. *The Mother's Almanac.* (Practical Parenting Books)

Klein, Carole. *The Single Parent Experience.* (Single Parents)

Kraus, Charles and Linda. *Charles the Clown's Guide to Children's Parties.* (Toys, Games, and Creative Learning Activities for Children)

La Leche League International. *The Womanly Art of Breastfeeding.* (Nutrition)

Lansky, Vicki. *Feed Me, I'm Yours.* (Nutrition)

Leach, Penelope. *Your Baby and Child.* (Basic Health and Child Development)

Leboyer, Frederick. *Loving Hands.* (Emotional Needs of Children and Parents)

Lerman, Saf. *Parent Awareness.* (Discipline and Childrearing Primers)

Levy, Janine. *The Baby Exercise Book.* (Cognitive and Motor Development)

Marzollo, Jean. *Supertot.* (Toys, Games, and Creative Learning Activities for Children)

Marzollo, Jean and Lloyd, Janice. *Learning Through Play.* (Toys, Games, and Creative Learning Activities for Children)

McBride, Angela Barron. *The Growth and Development of Mothers.* (Emotional Needs of Children and Parents)

Norris, Gloria and Miller, JoAnn. *The Working Mother's Complete Handbook.* (Two-Career Families)

Painter, Genevieve. *Teach Your Baby.* (Toys, Games, and Creative Learning Activities for Children)

Parke, Ross D. *Fathers.* (Fathers)

Patterson, Gerald R. *Living with Children.* (Discipline and Childrearing Primers)

Pogrebin, Letty Cottin. *Growing Up Free.* (Non-Sexist Childrearing)

Princeton Center for Infancy and Early Childhood. *The First Twelve Months of Life.* Frank Caplan, Ed. (Cognitive and Motor Development)

Princeton Center for Infancy. *The Parenting Advisor.* Frank Caplan, Ed. (Basic Health and Child Development)

Rozdilsky, Mary Lou and Banet, Barbara. *What Now? A Handbook for New Parents.* (The Transition to Parenthood)

Spock, Benjamin. *Baby and Child Care.* (Basic Health and Child Development)

Sullivan, S. Adams. *The Father's Almanac.* (Practical Parenting Books)

Thevenin, Tine. *The Family Bed.* (Emotional Needs of Children and Parents)

Weiss, Joan Soloman. *Your Second Child.* (Discipline and Childrearing Primers)

White, Burton L. *The First Three Years of Life.* (Cognitive and Motor Development)